BENCHLEY AT THE THEATRE

Dramatic Criticism, 1920-1940
by ROBERT BENCHLEY

Edited, and with an Introduction,
by CHARLES GETCHELL

THE IPSWICH PRESS
IPSWICH, MASSACHUSETTS 01938

GEMENTS

The editor wishes to express his gratitude to Robert Benchley's grandsons, Peter Benchley and Nathaniel Robert Benchley, for their authorization of this project; to *The New Yorker* for permission to reprint the reviews from that magazine; to Rodney Armstrong, Director and Librarian of the Boston Athenaeum, and his staff, as well as to Andrew Anspach, Managing Director of the Hotel Algonquin, for their kind assistance during the research phase; to Mary Ann Landsverk, for processing the words; and to Paulette, Nancy, Hazel, Sully, Judi and Susmita at Altertext, Boston, for the typesetting and make-up.

The jacket design is based on a drawing by Gluyas Williams which appeared in LIFE in 1925. The hand lettering is by Jon McIntosh.

The end-piece decorations were done by Fred G. Cooper, art editor of LIFE during the Benchley years there.

The review articles from LIFE were copyrighted © by Life Publishing Company in the years 1920 through 1929, both dates inclusive.

The review articles from *The New Yorker* were copyrighted © by The New Yorker Magazine, Inc., in the years 1929 through 1940, both dates inclusive; and all such copyrights were duly renewed.

Published by
THE IPSWICH PRESS
Box 291
Ipswich, Massachusetts 01938
ISBN 0-938864-05-X

CONTENTS

Introduction   ix

PART I
The Years at LIFE: 1920-1929

The Personal Service of Mr. Ed Wynn   3
"Heartbreak House"   5
Shaw on Over-Enthusiastic Audiences   7
So Deep!   9
"What, In Our House?"   11
Blacks in the Theatre   13
Rustlings of Spring   17
"Destroy the Audience!"   20
The Twenty-One Day Shaw-Cycle Race   22
Unbiased Criticism   24
Memories of Happy Days at the Follies   26
Berlin Letter   28
Was Shylock Really Hamlet?   30
Eddie Cantor and "Yes, We Have No Bananas"   33
The Marx Brothers   35
"Sweeney Todd, the Barber of Fleet Street"   37
An Open Letter to the Public   39
The Boy Who Grew Up   42
Two Ways   44
Labor Troubles   46
A Notable Revival   48
Paris Letter   50
Munich Letter   52
Vienna Letter   54

Budapest Letter 56

Announcing Defeat 58

Thistles from a Thistle Bush 60

Just a Touch of Heresy 63

Add Folk Plays 65

The Drama in Vienna 68

All About "Strange Interlude" 70

In the Vernacular 72

Junior Drama 75

Horreur! 78

Tryouts 80

New Resolutions 83

Harpo, Groucho, Chico, Zeppo and Karl 86

Turnabout 88

Old Wine 91

The Season's Peak 93

"Dynamo" 96

The Elephant Who Almost Forgot 98

PART II

The Years at *The New Yorker*: 1929-1940

Ex Post Facto 103

Satire to Music 106

What is a Good Show? 108

With Love from the Greek 111

Preliminary Lecture 113

Hurrah for Us! 115

Intermission 118

More Like It 121

"The Band Wagon" 124

How I Spent My Vacation 126

"Mourning Becomes Electra" 129

Questionnaire 132

Shavings from Shaw 135
Confessional 138
Top and Bottom 141
The Old Days 144
The Letter-Box 147
"Design for Living" 149
"The 3-Penny Opera" 152
"Night and Day" 155
Summing Up 157
Just "Roberta" 160
"The Lake" At Last 163
Good News 166
Statement 170
The Government Takes a Hand 172
"Idiot's Delight" 175
Big Names 178
Pro Flesh and Blood 180
"Tonight at 8:30" 183
Divided Opinion 185
"Babes in Arms" 188
Shakespeare Again 190
Two at Once 192
"The Sea Gull" 195
"The Boys from Syracuse" 197
Questions Without Answers 199
Going Overboard for Ethel Merman 201
"The Little Foxes" 203
Critics' Anniversaries 205
The Male and Allied Animals 207
One Thing and Another 209

Index 213

INTRODUCTION

In his last column as drama critic of the "old" LIFE magazine, in March of 1929, Robert Benchley expressed his outrage at having discovered, "quite by accident," after nine years on the job, that his deadline was really Wednesday night, not Tuesday. "For four hundred and sixty eight weeks," he complained, "we have been wearing our nerves to shreds in order to have everything in a whole day ahead of what was necessary. And they have been sitting here laughing at us."

The editor of the present volume, like Robert Benchley himself, is possessed of an antipathy to time schedules and an idiosyncratic notion of sport. His idea of a worthy contest is to let a deadline lead him right down to the wire, and then to pull away at the finish, to the astonishment of spectators. So it was that he found himself, scarcely a month before publication date, sitting on a beach in Brittany and wondering how he would do justice to the task of introducing this collection. (Being a lawyer by profession, he felt particularly daunted in the service of Robert Benchley, who has been described by his son Nathaniel as capable of "saying in a sentence what it took a lawyer ten minutes to say.")

Imagine then his delight at discovering—in one of last year's *New Yorkers*, which he had found on his bedroom table and was using as a paperweight on the sand—the remark that a book under review had not been "sullied with any bibliographical or biographical information, whether in the form of introduction, afterword or footnote." Very well, he said to himself, putting aside his notebooks and leaping into the sea; if unsullied is the fashion, unsullied it shall be! The passage of a topless windsurfer a few moments later, however, led him to reflect that perhaps a distinction had to be drawn between unsullied and conspicuously undressed. So he swam ashore, sharpened his pencil anew, and set about addressing his readers.

He imagines that they will fall into three categories. (This is not like a Chinese restaurant menu; any reader may opt for all three categories.) First, there are the theatre buffs. This is not a theatrical history, properly speaking, nor a comprehensive reference work; those are already available. It is instead a selection—here for the first time in book form—from the chronicles of a discerning critic who was on hand for hundreds of opening nights during two decades that can now be seen as a golden age of the American theatre. What made it a golden age? The playwrights, for one thing: Shaw, Galsworthy, Ervine, O'Neill, Barry, Coward, Connelly, Brecht, Bolton, Wodehouse, Lindsay, Crouse, Wilder, Hellman, Hart, Kaufman (as well as old-timers who were being revived with skill and imagination: Ibsen, Chekhov, Shakespeare). Then there were the players, from Ed Wynn and W. C. Fields to Orson Welles and Katharine Hepburn, by way of such stars as the Barrymores, Lunt and Fontanne, Helen Hayes, Maurice Evans, John Gielgud, Judith Anderson, Tallulah Bankhead, the Marx Brothers, Fred Astaire, Bea Lillie, Laurence Olivier, Ethel Merman, Fred Allen and Bob Hope.

The American musical comedy was outgrowing its origins in the European operetta, thanks to the work of Cohan, Kern, Hammerstein, the Gershwins, Rodgers and Hart, Dietz and Schwartz, Cole Porter and others. It was also an era of unusual creativity in stage and set design (Norman Bel Geddes, Robert Edmond Jones, Lee Simonson, Jo Mielziner) and in choreography (George Balanchine, Agnes de Mille).

Moreover, the economics of the theatre and the life of theatregoers—talking motion pictures did not arrive until the middle of the period, and television was of course far in the future—combined to motivate and reward the entrepreneurs and impresarios. As a group, the producers and directors are less celebrated than their authors, actors and composers, but among them such names as Florenz Ziegfeld, Jed Harris, Vinton Freedley and George Abbott stand out. The efforts of individual entrepreneurs came to be supplemented in time by innovations in production or finance on the part of groups, including the Theatre Guild, the Mercury Theatre, and the Federal Theatre Project. (These short lists of names risk being unfair. Just have a look at the index.)

To be sure, not everything in the theatre between the two world wars was golden. The quality floated on the top of a quantity of theatrical production that seems astounding today. During the 1930-31 season, for example, one hundred and ninety seven shows opened, many of which were mercifully short lived. For every "Mourning Becomes Electra," there were a couple of dozen like "Angeline Moves In," and one sympathizes with Benchley and his cohorts for having had to sit through—or at least show up for—all of them. Edmund Wilson, in an extract from his notebooks published posthumously under the title "The Twenties," suggests indeed that Benchley did not attend "at all" the shows he was reviewing for LIFE during a certain period. If that was so, in a way it's no wonder. But it's doubtful that, in twenty years on the beat, he missed any of the good ones.

For the social historians among you, Prohibition, the Jazz Age, the Depression, the New Deal, the gathering war clouds—all found their reflection in the contemporary theatre and its criticism. If you really want to get into that period, go to the public library and leaf through the bound volumes of LIFE and *The New Yorker* for those years—although prolonged immersion in that good-humored innocence can have a depressing effect in light of our knowledge of what was to come. It is astonishing, incidentally, to see from the cartoons and anecdotes what a broad range of targets sophisticated Americans considered fair game for teasing in those faraway days: blacks, Jews, the Irish, the Italians, Orientals, poor folk, farm folk, domestic servants, women automobile drivers. Benchley's pleas on behalf of blacks in the theatre in the 1920's appear incongruous in company with old LIFE cartoons poking fun at the illiteracy and alleged indolence of black people.

As a social critic, Robert Benchley was compassionate without being sentimental, and he was ahead of his time in many ways. He was active in the efforts to secure a new trial for Sacco and Vanzetti during the "red scare" of the twenties. As early as 1939, he was already wincing at the phrase "senior citizens." But his crystal ball was not infallible. In a 1929 review of "Wings Over Europe" (pages 93-94), he wrote that "when an author writes a play about blowing up the world by a redistribution of atoms he cannot expect to convince his audience any sooner than he could convince the Cabinet of Great Britain." (Why doesn't somebody look into reviving *that* play?)

The other category of readers is of course the phalanx of Robert Benchley fans. If you aren't one when you begin this book, you will be before you're very far into it, and you'll be bound to read the sixteen other Benchley collections, from "Of All Things" (1921) to "A Good Old-Fashioned Christmas" (1980), and to seek out his forty-six movie shorts, from "The Treasurer's Report" (Fox, 1928) to "I'm a Civilian Here Myself" (U. S. Navy, 1945), some of which are making a reappearance on cable television. For those of you who require it, we have organized a quick biographical tour, concentrating especially on the lesser-known years leading up to Benchley's career as a drama critic. You would be well advised, though, not to overlook the two excellent short biographies, which the editor gratefully acknowledges as the source of much of the information that follows here: "Robert Benchley," by his son Nathaniel, with a foreword by Robert E. Sherwood (McGraw-Hill, 1955), and "Robert Benchley: His Life and Good Times," by Babette Rosmond (Doubleday, 1970). These books have the slight inconvenience of being organized more or less thematically rather than chronologically, but the authors knew their subject and the books are animated with their affectionate understanding of him.

Robert Charles Benchley was born in 1889 in Worcester, Massachusetts, the son of the mayor's clerk and his wife, "a happily married couple, in a middle-class Victorian sort of way," as Nathaniel described them. The couple's only other child, a son named Edmund, was thirteen years older than Robert and was killed in the Spanish-American War. Edmund's fiancee, Lillian Duryea, of Nyack, New York, took young Robert under her wing and paid his way through a year of Phillips Exeter Academy and four years of Harvard, where he graduated with the class of 1912 and was president of the *Lampoon*. (One of his colleagues on the *Lampoon* was Gluyas Williams, who was to become the illustrator of Benchley's stories.) Then followed jobs at the Boston Museum of Fine Arts, as editor of a house organ for the Curtis Publishing Company, and as an employee welfare director for the Russell Paper Company in Boston.

All the while, Benchley was writing essays and short stories under the encouragement of Frank Crowninshield, editor of *The Century*. His first published free lance piece—a parody entitled "No Matter From What Angle You Look At It, Alice Brookhausen Was a Girl Whom You Would Hesitate to Invite Into Your Own Home"—appeared in 1914 in *Vanity Fair*, of which Crowninshield had become editor. In the spring of that year, Benchley married his childhood sweetheart, Gertrude Darling. At the end of 1915, just after the birth of Nathaniel, the Benchleys moved to New York, where Robert had been hired by Franklin P. Adams as a city reporter on the *Tribune*.

Benchley soon realized that he was not cut out for that line of work. Nathaniel attributes this realization to his father's reluctance "to ask people questions that he considered none of his business." So he welcomed Adams' invitation a few months later to move over to the staff of the *Tribune Magazine*. For the next year, he apparently enjoyed himself writing book reviews and weekly features about New York life. (The research for one of those features is recalled in "Confessional", pages 138-140.) In the evenings at home in the suburbs, he was doing free lance pieces for *Vanity Fair*. When the *Tribune Magazine* was discontinued in the summer of 1917, Benchley worked for a few months as press agent for an uncongenial Broadway producer. He followed this with a stint in Washington as press representative of the Aircraft Board. In the spring of 1918, Benchley accepted the offer of his friend Ernest Gruening, editor of the New York *Tribune* (later governor of Alaska) to become editor of its *Graphic* section, but in July Gruening was fired by the owners, who found his editorial policies insufficiently jingoistic, and Benchley resigned in protest. He then worked for nine months in the press section of the Liberty Loan, soliciting and placing articles in national magazines in support of Liberty Bonds.

In May of 1919, a few months before the birth of Robert, Jr., Frank Crownin-shield persuaded Condé Nast to hire Benchley at $100 a week as managing editor of *Vanity Fair*. His colleagues there included Robert E. Sherwood (drama editor, six feet seven inches tall) and Dorothy Parker (versifier and stand-in for P. G. Wodehouse as drama critic, barely five feet). This trio—who Nathaniel said resembled a "walking pipe organ" when they went down the street together—often lunched at the Hotel Algonquin. This was the genesis of the celebrated Algonquin Round Table group, whose antics have been recounted in numerous books and articles. Benchley, Sherwood and Parker were evidently too free-spirited for the rather stuffy Nast organization, with its intra-office policy memoranda and "tardy" slips, and in January of 1920 they all resigned.

After a few months as a free lance, operating out of an office cubbyhole he shared with Dorothy Parker in the Metropolitan Opera House studios, Benchley was given the sort of job he had been dreaming of: drama editor of Charles Dana Gibson's LIFE, at $100 for a thousand words a week and seven cents a word for anything else he did. He held this post for nine years, and the incidental "anything else" turned out to be the short humorous pieces which formed the core of the books that appeared every couple of years and helped make Benchley a national celebrity.

The decade of the twenties also saw the emergence of Robert Benchley the actor. For a one-night revue which the members of the Algonquin Round Table put together in April of 1922 to amuse their friends, Benchley made up a monologue parody called "The Treasurer's Report." Irving Berlin and Sam Harris happened to be in the audience, and they enlisted Benchley to appear in their next "Music Box Revue" for the handsome sum of $500 a week. The show played for nine months, and Benchley's eight-minute spot required him to miss very little of whatever shows he was reviewing for LIFE. He later did ten weeks on the road with the "Revue" in the Keith's vaudeville circuit.

"The Treasurer's Report" was made into the first all-talking motion picture by Fox in 1928. This marked the beginning of Benchley's other major career, that of film actor, and the inception of a conflict that would trouble him for years. He eventually appeared as the star in some forty-six shorts and as a supporting actor in nearly as many feature-length pictures. His film-making amused him, was not too demanding, and brought him unaccustomed financial rewards. But it also separated him from his family for long periods of time, and it distracted him from his writing. In 1928 and 1929 alone he made five films, and he finally felt constrained to give up his job at LIFE. The legitimate theatre continued to intrigue him, however, and late in 1929 he agreed to succeed Charles Brackett as drama critic of Harold Ross's *New Yorker*.

Benchley had been contributing occasional pieces to the magazine since 1925, and since 1927 had been producing a column for Ross called "The Wayward Press" under the pseudonym "Guy Fawkes." By all accounts, the *New Yorker* affiliation was a happy one. It lasted until 1940, and Benchley wrote many side pieces for the magazine in addition to his theatre reviews. His movie commitments took him frequently to Hollywood—he made twenty-five shorts during the thirties, nine of them in the year 1938 alone—and during his absences the *New Yorker* drama page was done by Dorothy Parker, E. B. White or Wolcott Gibbs. But Benchley begrudged his time away from Broadway. In October 1932 he wrote:

Teacher has been working in Hollywood for three months and is so goddam glad to see actors on a real stage and in real plays again that practically anything on which a curtain goes up and down is an event of almost insupportable excitement.

By the end of the decade, though, Benchley had begun to grow weary of the routine, which had now been complicated by his work in radio. His solution was to abandon his writing. He rationalized this with the contention that "no humorist is ever funny after the age of fifty." Nathaniel recalled those days in a conversation shortly before his own death with the writer Robert Luhn, whose account of their meeting appeared in *Book Forum* in 1982 ("Good Spirits: Robert Benchley Remembered"). The following extract is reproduced with Mr. Luhn's kind permission:

xiv

He became more and more irascible. Everything he did, every idea he had, he thought, 'Oh God, I did that in 1920.' Suddenly everything had a *déjà vu* quality about it. There was a *je m'en fiche* that crept over him. And I think some of that irascibility came from the approaching terminus, shall we say. Writing was just getting harder and harder. He showed me the last theatre column he did for *The New Yorker*, and asked me what I thought. I said it was splendid. 'Well,' he said, 'it was written in blood, I can tell you that.'

That last column—which is the last piece in this collection—appeared on January 27, 1940. Benchley made sixteen more short films and appeared in a number of feature movies, but his writing career was over. He died unexpectedly of a cerebral hemorrhage in New York on November 21, 1945. He was fifty-six years old.

We don't need to say much about the pieces in this collection; our readers should have the pleasure of making their own discoveries. But a few general observations will not be out of order. To begin with, it is evident that Robert Benchley was not an especially easy man to please. He did not go out of his way to be unkind—as we feel that Dorothy Parker may sometimes have done—but he did not hesitate to register his disappointment or disapproval. He was notably dismissive of anything he found tasteless, banal or prurient, whatever the box office said. During the 1931 season, for example, he was

shocked that leering little dabblings in the pools of sex, involving the services of such a nice little girl as Miss Margaret Sullavan, should draw down laughter from a New York audience which was supposedly preening itself on being sophisticated.

Later that year, he objected to a playwright's "scatological complex," and, reviewing Earl Carroll's "Vanities," he referred to "the clamflats of the world's dirtiest sketches (and when I say 'dirty,' I mean 'dirty,' for I am an old public school boy with a strong stomach)."

Benchley was relentlessly unpretentious, to the point of issuing periodic disclaimers, such as the one in his column of July 21, 1924 (pages 39-41):

A great many people seem to take this department seriously. They read the deathless little literary *bijoux* on this page, tossed off quite obviously for the enrichment of our national letters and for no other reason, and between the lines find a tacit assumption on our part that we expect them to follow our advice in the matter of choosing plays. . . . If, through years of checking up on our likes and dislikes in the theatre, you find that they correspond approximately to your own, then we have no objection to your taking a chance once in a while and gambling on a couple of seats on our tip. But if, out of a clear sky, you read something on this page (which is hereby proclaimed the most unreliable, inconsistent and temperamental page of personal reactions in the country), and on the strength of it go out and pay money for a show which you do not like, and *then* write an indignant letter blaming us, we give you fair warning now that we will have you arrested.

As Nathaniel put it, "he was reluctant to do anything that appeared to be straining to make the point." One guesses that Benchley may have felt that the art of the theatre, being a live cooperative enterprise created afresh for each audience, called for lighter and less dogmatic criticism than the non-performing arts. He never shrank from registering his judgment, but he often added, "I may be wrong." We were about to say what a wonderful teacher he would have been, but, come to think of it, he *was* a wonderful teacher.

If, as someone has said, a writer is someone on whom nothing is lost, then Robert Benchley was a writer *par excellence*. He had a knack of picking up the little bits that serve to illuminate the whole, and of depicting them with felicity. He seems to have taken infinite care with the polishing of his work. The reader is hard put to find a single awkward or slipshod sentence.

Finally, a word about how this collection was put together. Distilling twenty years' of criticism into a book of manageable proportions is not an easy task. The first rough cut eliminated reviews wherein neither the plays, playwrights nor players are much talked about today, unless the piece stands on its own merits as an example of Benchley humor. The second cut was more difficult, taking out many close "also rans." Nearly all of Benchley's theatre columns dealt with two or three shows, and many of the pieces here have been trimmed down to a single subject. In a few of those cases, they have been re-titled to avoid confusion, but most of them carry their original titles. The piece beginning on page 13 gathers together four items from a three-year period. Benchley would not have used the term "blacks" in those days, but we think he would prefer it today, so we put it in the title. There, as throughout the book, however, we have left the text itself unaltered.

This editor first encountered the Benchley books as a high school student, not long after the writer's death. He remembers withdrawing the collections from the public library, one by one, and reading them aloud with his friends during the long summer evenings. The day after they had finished the last one, and realized that there weren't any more, the world seemed very flat and dull indeed.

Well cheer up, friends. Here's more, after all!

CHARLES GETCHELL

PART I

THE YEARS AT *LIFE*
1920–1929

THE PERSONAL SERVICE
OF MR. ED WYNN

J UST as it was beginning to look as if no one was ever going to be really funny
again on the musical comedy stage, Ed Wynn brought his Carnival to the
New Amsterdam Theatre, and now everything is all right once more.

The Carnival in itself is very difficult to remember. There really is no Carnival
when Ed Wynn isn't on the stage (a total of perhaps four minutes during the
entire performance). It is true, there are some clever and amusing tumblers, Regal
and Moore, and a good jazz band, but over all we feel the tender and solicitous
presence of the master mind, Mr. Wynn. He hovers about in and out of the wings,
across the back of the stage, even in the lobby, wishing the departing audience
good night; watching with apprehension the acts of his colleagues, giving apologetic advice here and a motherly warning there, calling the attention of his
patrons to such items as he considers especially good or bad, and, in general,
being continually in the way and very ineffective.

Of course, this personal-service feature was originally Raymond Hitchcock's,
when he stood in the aisle welcoming the audience by name as they took their
seats. But Ed Wynn's personal service is not an imitation of Mr. Hitchcock's. It is
distinctly his own. He has Mr. Hitchcock's solicitous interest in the performance,
without Mr. Hitchcock's *savoir faire*. He is never quite at ease about the thing.
There is a constant nervousness for fear that you won't understand, or that you
will think it trivial. He has so many cares in running the rest of the show that it is a
wonder that he can find time to do his own work, and yet he appears in elaborate
character roles throughout the piece, representing in turn a lightning calculator, a
juggler, a stage hand, a violinist and an eccentric dancer, besides maintaining the
continuous role of impresario.

He also wrote the piece, although he admits (in a gigantic announcement on the
drop curtain before the play begins) that he had great trouble in doing the lyrics,
owing to the difficulty of finding a word to rhyme with "orange."

3

Ed Wynn is coming into his own as one of the few really funny men on the American stage. His appeal is difficult to analyze, but he has that same aura of pathos which sublimates Charlie Chaplin and makes him by turns a great comedian and a great tragedian.

Ed Wynn never quite attains what he sets out after. His waistcoat is always buttoned just one or two buttons too high. His clothes, while perhaps suitable for other occasions, are never quite right for the particular event in which he is taking part. (An ulster and a size-8 derby, for instance, worn while directing a dainty dance of dream girls, or a fez and white duck knickerbockers in the Colosseum at Rome.) His language, while he has no trouble with pronunciation and chooses words which are, as words, impeccable, is always just a shade too refined or rather badly assembled, so that the general effect is one of undeniable failure. And his property jokes, in spite of solicitous nurturing and careful editing, are always duds. He tries so hard, and is so eager to please, that his failures might well call for tears from a sympathetic audience, if it was not so busy laughing. But, for once, Ed Wynn has not fallen short of his goal. He has tried to produce a good entertainment in his Carnival, and he has unquestionably succeeded.

May 6, 1920

"HEARTBREAK HOUSE"

A GREAT deal of unnecessary worry is indulged in by theatregoers trying to understand what Bernard Shaw means. They are not satisfied to listen to a pleasantly written scene in which three or four clever people say delightful things, but they needs must purse their lips and scowl a little and debate as to whether Shaw meant the lines to be an attack on monogamy as an institution or a plea for manual training in the public school system.

"Heartbreak House" unquestionably has a message, but I doubt if it is worth as much as the dialogue. The characters quite probably represent different types which are significant as a commentary on English social and political life; but even if you have never heard of English social and political life, they are delicious simply as characters. And their presentation by the members of the Theatre Guild, assisted by such charming ringers as Elizabeth Risdon, Lucille Watson and Effie Shannon, is all that could be asked.

What there is of the story deals with a throng of aimless guests who move in a mad manner about the commodious house of a retired sea-captain in Sussex. One feels during the first act that, if everyone continues to be as delightful as they then are, the play might well run on forever without any final curtain. This wish is nearly fulfilled in the second act, which is just twice as long as any act has a right to be. But everything is brought to a happy ending in the last scene by three of the loudest explosions ever heard on any stage, with the possible exception of that which occurred in the Opera House in St. Petersburg in 1891, when the royal box containing the Grand Duke Sergius and family was blown out into the Nevskii Prospekt.

Just as after hearing an opera by Victor Herbert I always feel extremely graceful and confident that, with any encouragement at all, I could dance divinely across the concourse of the Grand Central Terminal, I always feel very clever after a

Shaw play. I think that I look clever, too. It seems as if people must notice it, even before I speak. And when I finally bring myself to utter something like, "A good show, wasn't it?" to a friend on the way out, I do it with a twinkle in my eye and a droll expression to my mouth, as if I were standing with a gardenia in my buttonhole and a cup of tea in my hand, saying something enormously witty and cynical to the Countess of Deerfoot.

Perhaps that is why I enjoy Shaw so much, and why I could sit through "Heartbreak House" all over again, even the second act and the explosions.

December 9, 1920

SHAW ON OVER-ENTHUSIASTIC AUDIENCES

I T IS too long a story to tell how it came about that this department got into communication with George Bernard Shaw. I will therefore tell it.

A letter from Mr. Shaw has just arrived commenting on remarks made in these columns anent an over-enthusiastic audience spoiling the performance of a play by ill-timed applause. Quoting from the Shaw letter in an offhand manner:

"I wish you would start a campaign against the interruption of plays by applause and laughter. Imagine an orchestral symphony stopped every three bars or so by the audience brawling their delight at a pretty progression or a rousing fortissimo, as operas are interrupted in Italy. I have had performances of my plays prolonged for twenty-five minutes beyond the rehearsal time by incontinent hee-hawings from the very people who complain afterwards that they had to leave before the end to catch their trains. As to acting, it is impossible under such circumstances, except by snatches. I have twice appealed to the London public to treat my plays as sensibly as they treat Wagner's music dramas, and not make a noise until the curtain is down."

With but slight attempt to conceal the inordinate pride felt by this department at having been designated from No. 10 Adelphi Terrace to carry on the American end of the anti-audience campaign, let it be stated that nothing could be nearer our departmental heart.

Why should a critic spend all his time picking flaws with people on the stage, when fully as much harm is being done to the cause of the drama by the rabble in dinner jackets and evening gowns out front?

They have paid their good money and they are going to get it back in trade. So they loudly applaud every line that pleases them, evidently on the theory that if they make enough noise it will be repeated in a few minutes for their benefit. They hold up the performance when their favorite star enters, and prevent anyone from speaking a line until they have expressed their feelings to the utmost by beating the palms of their hands together. They think that practically everything in the play is funny, and laugh accordingly. If they happen to like a song or a dance, they make it impossible for the piece to go on until they have gorged themselves with encores. And the worst of it is, they smile in a knowing manner as they do it, showing that it is deliberate. They even look about them for approval.

And then, of course, there are the coughers. This department will continue to wage war against them until every bronchial sufferer exercises his unquestioned prerogatives under the Constitution and stays home from the theatre.

In fact, the theatre would be much better off if everyone, with the exception of me and a few of my friends, stayed at home. And even then I should like to go alone once in a while.

December 23, 1920

SO DEEP!

A PARTICULARLY beautiful performance by Margaret Wycherly makes it worth while to totter 'way down to the Bramhall Playhouse and see "Mixed Marriage." It is one of those Irish plays, by St. John Ervine, in which there is a great deal of "tay" drunk, and where everything is either "quare an' fine" or "quare an' bad." A large amount of coarse breadstuffs is consumed in hungry peasant fashion during the four acts, also. But, for all this, it is a drama of considerable power.

The family around whom the play centers seem to be the Belfast branch of the John Fergusons, an impression which is heightened by the presence in the cast of Augustin Duncan (he that was *John Ferguson*) and Rollo Peters, still calling his stage father "Daa." It makes no difference to Mr. Peters whether his father's name is *John Ferguson* or *John Rainey*. He is always "Daa" to Rollo.

But Mr. Peters gives an effective performance, and so do most of the cast. The play itself, thanks largely to Miss Wycherly's interpretation, is magnificent in spots. In others, it becomes simply an Irish peasant play in which loquacious Catholics and Protestants follow each other in and out the door (at left) saying that it really doesn't make any difference in which church you worship so long as your harp is in the right place. There seems to be one act too many in the piece, and, if I wanted to be personal, I should say that it is the third. In order that there shall be no mistake, everything in that act is said three times.

The whole play is, however, sufficiently important and interesting to dispossess at least one of the plays now occupying Broadway theatres. (One would be enough.)

The unpleasant thing about a play by St. John Ervine, or Galsworthy or Shaw, is that they attract to the theatre so many "bravo" murmurers. They are usually ladies, and whenever a line is spoken on the stage which they consider especially significant or true, they murmur "bravo" to themselves.

They do it very gently, of course, but with so much intensity and depth of emotional power that it reaches those sitting within a radius of twelve seats. This shows that they are getting it. Sometimes they simply make indistinct crooning sounds in their throats, as if to say: "How little anyone except St. John and myself appreciates the truth of that!" But usually it is "bravo," especially if the line has been well delivered. Once in a while you will find a daring linguist who comes across with a "brava" instead of "bravo." But this is likely to be saved until the end of an act, and is accompanied by applause in which the hands are held high and at arm's length from the body. But anyone may do anything that he pleases at the end of an act.

Thus, in "Mixed Marriage," when Miss Wycherly says something like: "Sure, an' 'tis quare an' bitter th' life we wimmin lead," there arises from the audience a sound like an offstage mob coming in the distance. It is the ladies indicating that they get the meaning of the line. It might be simpler if, after a good significant remark, the actor were to step to the footlights and say: "Will all those who understand what I have just said and who agree, please hold up their hands?" It certainly would be less noisy.

January 6, 1921

"WHAT, IN OUR HOUSE?"

ONLY those people will be allowed to read this little piece on "Macbeth" who will first admit that they are bored during two-thirds of most Shakespearean performances. We might just as well come out in the open about it.

Shakespeare is all right bound in limp leather, pocket-size, for personal use under a reading lamp, where you can skip or go back and reread, but when recited by a company of players for two hours at a stretch, most of the spoken words of the Immortal Bard are like so many drops of rain on a tin roof to this particular member of the *intelligentsia*. Julia Marlowe has the unique distinction of being the only living actress who has kept me awake throughout an entire performance of Shakespeare.

In Arthur Hopkins' production of "Macbeth" there was a slight incentive to keep awake just to see what the next scene was going to be, or, rather, what the next scene was *not* going to be. Scenery was abolished for the occasion, with the exception of one or two pieces which looked as if they had been abandoned in mid-stage by panicky scene-shifters caught by the sudden rising of the curtain. Once in a while a really beautiful drop curtain was lowered, taking the place of the drop used in vaudeville showing the corner of Main and Front Streets and moving vans. Then, in the banquet scene, some mossbacked conservative went out and got a lot of real candles, the only properties used during the performance which the audience could recognize, and they were greeted with a round of applause for old time's sake.

A word in the matter of ancient Scottish psychic phenomena as revealed by the presence of Banquo's ghost. Heaven knows why any ghost should want to visit such a banquet in the first place, for the impression given by the revellers was one of a coroner's jury invited in to see the King go mad, and very tired of waiting for it to happen.

11

But there the ghost came, nevertheless, and a very robust ghost he was, too. If you hadn't known the play you might have thought it was the night clerk paging Mr. Macbeth. It ambled in, looked about, and then quite naturally decided that there would be more fun back with the other ghosts who weren't afraid to admit that they were dead. So it executed a rather precarious backward march (one of the cleverest bits of acting in the play, for there were lots of things it might have tripped over), and disappeared.

As for the rest of the settings, the idea seemed to have been to have just one or two odd pieces standing around, one of them to be crooked. The whole was illuminated by the clearly distinguishable shafts from three or four spotlights concealed in the shirt fronts of members of the orchestra, giving the familiar effect of a Hudson River town being picked on by the searchlight of the Albany night-boat.

You will instantly see that all this symbolized the involuntary degradation of two souls caught in the meshes of a perverse destiny. Sometimes the symbolism was so strong that it didn't seem as if it could be borne any longer. In fact, several people had to leave early. Others covered their eyes with their hands and had to be roused when the thing was over.

"Macbeth" without scenery might be well enough, but "Macbeth" without scenery and without acting really leaves nothing much to take hold of. Lionel Barrymore growled consistently through *Macbeth's* varying emotions, suggesting in appearance a slightly intoxicated Norseman. Julia Arthur gave a very refined combination performance of *Lady Macbeth* and *Juliet*. Both seemed under the impression that the *Macbeths* were an eminently respectable couple (*Mr. Macbeth* a little moody when in drink, perhaps) who were given to walking in their sleep and doing the strangest things to their guests. You feel that all concerned will have a good, hearty laugh over the whole affair the next morning at the breakfast table.

The Hopkins theory, as nearly as can be ascertained, was to eliminate all nonessential things from the stage and the acting, leaving Shakespeare in the essence. Unfortunately they left the eliminator on too long, and not even Shakespeare was left.

March 10, 1921

12

BLACKS IN THE THEATRE

THIS department should not attempt to handle news events. Our announcement last week that the New York Drama League had decided not to ask Charles Gilpin to its dinner because he is a Negro appeared about a week after he had received a perfectly formal invitation from the League's secretariat, accompanied by urgent appeals to attend from individual members.

This sudden enthusiasm for Mr. Gilpin followed the newspaper publicity on the matter, publicity which aroused what is generally referred to as "a storm of protest" against the League's proposed discrimination. However fearful the dinner committee may have been originally concerning possible complications arising from Mr. Gilpin's presence, the very probable complications arising from his being barred were made too obvious to be ignored. If the publicity given the matter has been by any chance unfair to the Drama League, it has at least served the very good purpose of calling the matter to the attention of all future dinner committees.

March 30, 1921

* * *

THIS department has several times added its plea to those of others for a wider opportunity for the Negro in our theatre. Such native talent as is always uncovered when Negroes like Charles Gilpin or Opal Cooper are given a chance, and which is evident even in the superficial work done in the

13

Negro musical revues which have sprung into popularity this season, emphasizes the waste of confining men and women of this race to parts calling for nothing more ambitious than the strumming of a banjo or a comic acquiescence to the orders of "young Mars' Spencer."

It is encouraging, therefore, to find that in Howard University a movement is under way for the establishment of a national Negro Theatre where "the Negro playwright, musician, actor, dancer and artist in concert shall fashion a drama that shall merit the respect and win the admiration of the world." The work is under the direction of Montgomery Gregory, a young Negro graduate of Harvard, who is at the head of the Department of Dramatics at Howard, while Cleon Throckmorton, technical director of the Provincetown Players of New York, is instructor in such subjects as the designing and painting of scenery.

Since it has not been done for them, the Negroes are taking the matter of their contribution to the American theatre into their own hands, and, from a general survey of the field in New York, one comes to the conclusion that, after all, it could hardly have been placed in hands more promising.

November 3, 1921

* * *

THE regular dramatic reviewer of the "The Liberator" being unable to attend, Claude McKay went to cover the Theatre Guild's production of "He Who Gets Slapped." Claude McKay is an editor of "The Liberator" and a poet of distinction. He was accompanied by William Gropper, the artist.

Gropper got the passes at the box office and the two started for their seats. The usher looked at them, muttered something about seeing the manager, and taking their stubs with him left them standing in the aisle. In a moment he returned with the manager, who explained that the date was wrong or that it was raining outside or something equally relevant, and gave them, in place of their orchestra seats, two in the balcony.

The reason that they could not sit in the orchestra was that Claude McKay is a Negro.

This is, of course, New York's customary treatment of Negroes. It is nothing new. In the South they are at least frank about their discrimination. There is no pretense. In New York, which makes claims to being a modern community, such hypocrisy just makes things worse. And for the Theatre Guild, which above all producing bodies in this city snaps a delicate finger at commercialism in the name of the universality of art, even to condone the shunting of a writer of beautiful verse into the balcony of the theatre because he happens to be colored, would be comic were it not so terribly tragic.

May 25, 1922

* * *

THE production of "All God's Chillun Got Wings," long dreaded by the champions of Nordic supremacy and the guardians of the honor of white womanhood, has taken place, and, at a late hour last night, white women were still as safe on the streets of New York as they ever were and the banner of purity still floated from the ramparts of our own Caucasian stronghold. All that had happened was that a rather long and wordy play, with a powerful idea behind it, had been performed at the Provincetown Theatre, and that a Negro actor named Paul Robeson had taken his place with Charles Gilpin as one of the artists to whom his race may point with pride.

Miss Mary Blair, the white actress over whose honor there was so much vicarious worry, seemed to bear up very well under the ignominy of having to kiss the hand of a Negro gentleman, and gave by far the best performance of her career.

The audience at the opening, far from rising in protest, behaved better and evinced more intelligence than any audience we have ever seen. The following phenomena will show what we mean by "intelligence":

15

They did not laugh when slang was spoken on the stage.

They did not giggle at profanity.

They did not applaud the offstage singing of popular songs.

There was only one laugh drawn down by a character's saying that he had lived in Brooklyn, and that came, oddly enough, from the companion of one of our leading aesthetes. And she may have been laughing at something else.

June 5, 1924

RUSTLINGS OF SPRING

I N THE current edition of the circus now at Madison Square Garden one is chiefly impressed by the dispirited behavior of the elephants. The combination of world conditions and the theatrical slump seems to have depressed them.

They dance, it is true, but not with the same snap and verve that used to mark their performance. "Doris," the *première danseuse* of the troupe, goes through the formal motions of the one-step, and although she is much better at it than her trainer, her mind is quite obviously not on her work. Love might perhaps be at the bottom of this individual abstraction, but certainly the entire group of what are known in the patois of the circus as "performing pachyderms" cannot have fallen in love all at once, and the air of detachment appears general. It simply must be listed among the emotional reactions indicative of the great unrest which is sweeping the world.

It is gratifying to note, however, that at the climax of one of the stupendous group formations, the top elephant unfurls the Stars and Stripes, thereby putting the whole troupe on record as one hundred per cent American. It would be a terrible thing if the performing pachyderm element in the country were to go red.

Aside from the elephants, the circus seems about the same. There is this year, however, no magnificent introductory pageant depicting the triumphal entry of Nebuchadnezzar into Tyre (I know he didn't), but the entire company marches around the arena once, which is about all you could ask. Neither is there any single smashing, nerve-racking feature in which a man on a bicycle drops from the top of a tower into a basin of water. The omission of these departments is doubtless due to the general return to normalcy counselled by our new President (his name has slipped me for the moment).

The chief performer, for whom the arena is cleared and the lights lowered, and in whose behalf the drummer rolls an awe-inspiring prelude, is "Mlle. Leitzel, Queen of Aerial Gymnasts, who will amaze you with her wonderful feats of strength and endurance. Suspended at dizzy heights, this Miniature Marvel of the Air breaks every law of gravity, casting her body over her own shoulders scores of times without pause!"

That's right. She does it. That is, she casts her body over her own shoulders scores of times without pause. Just how many of the laws of gravity this violates will have to be judged by someone who knows how many different laws of gravity there are. One is all that comes to mind just at this moment, and Mlle. Leitzel avoids breaking the letter of this, whatever she does to its spirit, by always managing to keep a tight hold on something or other.

And, after all, when you have cast your body over your own shoulders scores of times without pause, what has been gained by it? You simply have cast your body over your shoulders scores of times without pause, and then you trip lightly to your dressing room. Of course, Mlle. Leitzel incidentally collects a substantial check from the P.T. Barnum estate, which must in part make up to her for the comparative futility of her calling in the great march of the world's progress.

Others of the more unimportant features are the wood-chopping contest and the living statuary. In the wood-chopping contest two men, evidently representing Harvard and Yale respectively, chop through the trunks of two large trees at what is probably high speed in tree-chopping circles. As a contest, however, it lacks a certain variety essential to keeping the spectators on their toes. And although Harvard's generalship and skillful chopping finally overcame the bulldog grit and moral earnestness of Yale, there was a suspicion, as there always is in contests which are a part of a nightly program, that the choppers were really good friends after all and that the affair was fixed beforehand.

The living statuary has not changed much in all these decades, and the participants, grown white in the service, still give startlingly unreal representations of the more prominent seasons of the year. The group entitled "Spring" has been made doubly effective this time by the insertion of multicolored electric lights in the vegetables and fruits; and according to the program the center group contains Miss Ena Claren, "known thoughout Europe as the Perfect Venus." With all that Europe has on its mind today, this is no small distinction.

The way to go to the circus, however, is with someone who has seen perhaps one theatrical performance before in his life and that in the High School hall. In such company you gradually find yourselves marveling in unison that a man can even stand up on a moving horse's back and gasping at the very idea of a woman swinging in the most elementary maneuvers from a trapeze. The scales of sophistication are struck from your eyes and you see in the circus a gathering of men and women who are able to do things as a matter of course which you couldn't do if your life depended on it. And that's a rather salutary experience every once in a while. It keeps you in your place.

April 14, 1921

"DESTROY THE AUDIENCE!"

THIS department has always maintained that the chief trouble with the theatre today is the audience. A futile warfare has been waged here against the coughers, the crooners, the nine o'clock arrivals, and, above all, the people who go to the theatre to be amused and therefore feel that they must get their money's worth of laughs, whether the script calls for laughs or not.

It needed, however, the intrepid terseness of Mr. Gilbert Seldes, writing in *The Dial*, to formulate a slogan which we should have been afraid to be the first to utter but to which we subscribe with all the vigor that is left in these old bones after a series of devitalizing defeats.

"Destroy the audience!" rings out the voice of Cato Seldes. "Everything else will follow."

Until this magnificently inclusive plan was suggested, our goal had been merely the elimination of most of the women from the audience by a thorough test of the reflexes of each patron entering the lobby. Each one should be placed in a darkened cabinet and the word "hell" or "damn" should suddenly be shouted at her. If she laughs or giggles, her money should be immediately refunded and she should be told to go down the street to the Columbia Burlesque.

It is perhaps unfair to say that women laugh oftener at the wrong place than men, but a careful observation of this type of play-wrecker brings one to the conclusion that women are more startled than men at the words "damn" and "hell" or any frank remark made on the stage, and that when some women are startled in this manner they emit a nervous giggle, even though the words are uttered at the deathbed of the heroine or the scaffold of the hero.

Certain it is that the laughter is predominantly feminine in those cases where laughter inflicts a deep wound on the spirit of the play. They laugh when *Liliom* slaps his little daughter's hand; they laugh when *Lady Kitty* in "The Circle" looks at the old photograph album; they laugh when *Anna Christie* tells of her life as a prostitute and whenever the old woman of the waterfront takes a drink; they think that one of the funny moments of "Kiki" is when the little girl puts on her tawdry costume to go out again into the streets of Paris, and, in "Main Street," they can hardly control themselves when *Doc Kennicott* is shown in his pajamas getting into bed during one of the most impressive scenes done in New York this winter. Anything spoken in Irish brogue or by a drunken man is funny and, of course, anything said by a character who was funny in the first act must necessarily be funny throughout the play. It has been estimated that the average powers of discrimination in a matinee audience in New York City would, if stood on end, not quite fill a demitasse. In most other cities you could get them in the saucer. And in any evening audience, including *men* and women, they wouldn't bulk impressive enough to send to any World's Fair as an exhibit.

The blame in the matter of coughing is by no means on the women. Here the men assert their rights, and having a more raucous tonality at their command, completely dominate the situation. But we have used up all our departmental vituperation writing in previous issues about the myriad native sons and daughters of Cougher Prairie. There is nothing more that we can say, except to point with pride to the agitation which is reported to have been started in French theatres against what our competitor, Mr. Nathan, might call the "bronchial boobery" and to join hands with Mr. Seldes in his anti-audience crusade for the betterment of our national theatre. It would be much better if plays could be presented before a selected audience consisting of me and a few of my friends.

December 22, 1921

THE TWENTY-ONE DAY
SHAW-CYCLE RACE

B Y THE time this bulletin appears, members of the Theatre Guild and its plucky audiences will be staggering forward on the third and last lap of the trek across "Back to Methuselah."

(For the benefit of those readers who do not follow the sporting news carefully, it should be explained that the Guild, in spite of the fact that there is no state law compelling it to produce Shaw's longest and dullest play, has divided it into three parts for production, one to be played each week until exhaustion sets in.)

Being able to write only of the first week of the cycle we are under a handicap, as it is impossible to tell whether the remaining weeks will produce anything so tiresome as the Garden of Eden scene or so amusing as the Lloyd George-Asquith bout of the first installment. From a reading of the play in book form, however, we should like to place five dollars on the dull.

The only thing that may upset these calculations is the genius of Mr. Lee Simonson for turning water into wine, using only a backdrop and a few pieces of scenery. Cotton Mather's "Magnalia" might be made emotionally thrilling for the first three or four hours if read aloud in front of a Simonson setting.

The chief trouble with a Shaw play is the Shaw enthusiasts in the audience. I am a Shaw enthusiast myself, but so long as I have control of my vocal organs it shall be a secret between the readers of this paper and me. People seem to come from miles around to a Shaw play feeling in duty bound to murmur, "Isn't that delightful?" to each other whenever the author uses the subjunctive mood.

If they would only save their murmuring and crooning for those passages of the play which even the author intended to be "delightful," but so afraid are they of having it thought that they are not getting the shades of meaning in the lines, that they take a chance on everything that sounds suspicious.

In the Garden of Eden scene in "Back to Methuselah" (which anyone, by reading the text, can discover contains nothing that has not been said in Garden of Eden scenes since Cain killed Abel for writing the first one) *Adam* says in effect to the *Serpent*:

"Give me a word which means 'I will do that tomorrow.'"

And the *Serpent* answers: "Procrastination."

At this almost terrifying selection of *le mot juste* a low moan of intense appreciation runs through the house and several ladies faint. Heaven knows what a really good one would do to them.

But even the devotees' desire to be considered hep to inside British politics, evidenced by screams of immoderate delight at every line spoken by the politicians *Joyce-Burge* and *Lubin*, cannot spoil the remarkable characterization of Lloyd George by A.P. Kaye and the hardly less deceptive Asquith of Claude King. Having never seen either of these statesmen, I am in a position to state that the caricatures are practically perfect. In fact, the whole scene in which the Gospel of the Brothers Barnabas is set forth is interesting enough to make it worthwhile leaving a call at the box office to be awakened at 10:15, in time to see it.

March 16, 1922

UNBIASED CRITICISM

CONSIDERABLE fault was found last year at this department's unsympathetic review of the circus. The burden of the complaint was that we see so many shows that we are incapable of viewing an elementary performance like this with anything but a jaundiced eye and hence our quibbling about the elephants' lethargy and the futility of Mlle. Leitzel's turning over and over on a rope in midair.

This year, therefore, we have delegated the work of reviewing Messrs. Barnum and Bailey to a less sophisticated member of the family who, in six years, has been to the Hippodrome twice and the Chauve-Souris once, but who has had sufficient circus experience to furnish a basis for critical comparison and an eye for values undilated by either surprise or terror.

Following is a report of the proceedings, translated and adapted for publication purposes, but in emphasis and commentary substantially as he submitted it to us over the oatmeal that evening.

First and foremost among the artistic features of the show was an automobile which fell apart disclosing a pig in it. This was beyond all doubt the crowning achievement of centuries and centuries of circus endeavor. Nothing like it has ever been seen or heard of, at least not so far as the written records show. The very recalling of it brought on such spasms of mirth that for a time it looked as if the review were to end here.

Quiet having been restored, it transpired that there were other features. Statues of horses (it was rumored that they were *real* horses making believe that they were statues, but this hardly seemed probable as they stood so still), with a big star in the center on which appeared the time. Here the report became a little confused. The relation of the star to the horses was not made quite clear, and repeated and sympathetic questioning brought out no good reason for the time's appearing in the tableau at all. The whole thing, as reported, had a beautiful intangibility which suggested that Maeterlinck may have written the act. Whoever wrote it, its symbolism didn't get over very big.

Then there seems to have been a girl with red hair who had her nurse with her to hold her coat. The presence of the nurse was so astounding as to obliterate any memory of what the girl with the red hair did after she had removed her coat. It is presumed that she did *something*, however, as everyone in the circus has to do *something*.

In the meantime, it must not be forgotten that there was the automobile which fell apart with the pig in it.

Favorable mention was made of two fat people with doors in their suits (this is authentic, as it was repeated under cross-examination several times without any serious discrepancy in detail) and from these doors fox terriers jumped out. The whole thing sounds fishy, and it is possible that we were being taken on for a sucker, but that is the way it was told to us in all apparent sincerity and we are bound to believe it.

There was also a man who tipped over in a chair who was pretty funny.

Considerable acting had to be done to demonstrate the particular virtues of the number in which cowboys appeared on horses. One of these horses, said to be called a "bucking bronco," threw his rider off and ran over him, the cowboy rolling himself up into a ball to escape injury. In showing how this was done, our reporter overturned a chair which gouged a large nick from the corner of the sideboard and sent his younger brother into gales of laughter. Encouraged by his success in this, it seemed best to him to repeat the act, until even his younger brother was satiated and everyone else had left the room in disgust.

April 13, 1922

MEMORIES OF HAPPY
DAYS AT THE FOLLIES

MR. ZIEGFELD'S having reduced the price of admission to his Follies this year makes it a little harder to be nasty about the show. It is worth less than it was last year, but as you are asked to pay less, it really brings you right back to where you started from. Except that, by the time you are through with the ticket agency, you will have spent a tidy sum, and a tidy sum of any size seems too much for what is offered. Here again, however, Mr. Ziegfeld's having sent this department free seats cramps our vituperativeness in this respect.

Leaving money out of the question, then, let us see what there is to pay you for your time.

It is customary to say that the Follies are beautiful to look at. All right, they are beautiful, especially the scenes and costumes designed by young Mr. James Reynolds. The girls, too, are pictorially effective, although they never look very clubby. I may be funny that way, but I like a little radiation of some sort in my beauty, and the Follies showgirls radiate at about the same degree Fahrenheit as Cleopatra's Needle. That's one reason I never went after Dolores stronger. She must have wondered what on earth was the matter with me that I never called her up or wrote to her.

Granted that the Follies are gorgeous to look at, then. After an hour or so your eyes get numb, and from then on Mr. William A. Brady might as well be producing the show. Unfortunately you can't do as you do with Nature whenever your eyes get tired of looking at the Grand Canyon or the Engadine Valley—stoop over and look upside down between your knees. The seats at the New Amsterdam would never allow for that. You *can* tip your head at right angles and get a new sort of view that way, but you are likely to be misunderstood by the people behind you and asked to leave the theatre.

We now come to the comedy. Right away it should be said that the absence of Fannie Brice and W.C. Fields started us out with a bias against the show. It didn't seem right to call it "The Follies" without them. We sat there, fairly glowing with ill will from the time the curtain went up, and not even Will Rogers could make us feel that the gap had been filled.

Now Will Rogers' own mother couldn't have cared more for him than we do, and we will laugh at practically anything he says, because he says it so ingratiatingly. But fifteen minutes of Will Rogers, delightful as they are, can't make up for those golden hours of the dear past when Fannie Brice sang and Fields fretted over the Ford in company with the grimly silent little man in the duster.

Great sobs shook our frame at these memories while we sat and listened to Mr. Gallagher and Mr. Shean sing about belligerent wives raising lumps on their husbands' heads, women getting the vote, and Prohibition. (Incidentally, it seems incredible that two comedians could start out with such a comic idea as that which forms the basis of the Gallagher and Shean song and reduce it so utterly to a banality by the introduction of a five-and-ten cent store lyric.)

Further tears, and real ones, were shed during the "Burlesk-Ballet" participated in by Nervo and Knox. Not that they didn't do it well enough, but that dance was a Dooley dance, and each time there was a crash of falling bodies we expected to see the little, impassive Dooley rise from the wreckage and glide heavily onward. But the little, impassive Dooley is dead, and we rather resent anyone else's trying to take his place—for a while, at any rate.

Ring Lardner has written a couple of skits for the show which do much to make the comedy bearable, especially the scene at the ball grounds in which Andrew Toombes and Will Rogers give startling representations of a couple of Yanks warming up. But when you consider all that you have to sit through before and after you come to the Lardner and Rogers episodes in the way of young ladies stepping to the footlights and reciting sweetly, "I am Miss Calculate" and "I am Miss Demeanor," drunken dancing, Hula-Hula girls shaking themselves in the manner which was calculated to throw the male element into a frenzy back in the days when "I'll tell the world" was new slang, with musical numbers entitled, "Throw Me a Kiss," "South Sea Moon," "Bring on the Girls" and "Hello, Hello, Hello!" you realize that, after all, there is nothing like canoeing for a summer evening.

June 29, 1922

BERLIN LETTER

Berlin, July 10th

IN ORDER to write a really scholarly review of the Berlin dramatic season, one ought to be able to catch more than one German word out of a hundred and fifty as they fly past. The last card I turned in gave my average as one in every hundred and ninety-three.

Following is about all that I got out of a charming performance of "*Der Kinder-Mörder*" ("The Child Killer") at the A.H. Woods Schauspielhaus.

The rising of the curtain discloses a room in what seems to be the Rugs, Draperies and Linoleum Department of John Wanamaker's. To make things harder for you, there is a pump in the center.

Friedel, the boy, is sitting by the pump talking with *Minna*, the girl. They talk a great deal about one thing and another. During the course of the conversation, *Friedel* says "*zimmer*," so the inference is that they are planning to take a room somewhere.

About five minutes after Friedel has said "*zimmer*," a man comes in who wants Friedel either to come downstairs or try on a new suit. Whatever it is he wants, *Friedel* says "*Nein*." This means that he won't do it. Good for *Friedel*!

But just at this moment an old woman comes in and dies. Several other people come in and kid back and forth, and after this has been going on for some time, one of them lets fall the word "*löffel*." It would seem, therefore, that the conversation has been brought around to the subject of spoons. This is considered a dramatic enough situation to bring the curtain down on.

The second act is laid in a charcoal burner's hut in the Black Forest. The charcoal burner comes in and says to his wife that it is cold outside. You can tell that he is saying this because he rubs his hands together before hitting her. She dies in the fireplace just as *Friedel* rushes in saying something about "*winter*," doubtless that the nights are longer in winter than they are in summer. He is followed by *Minna*, and they lie down on the floor together and talk in German for twenty minutes or half an hour, occasionally striking each other.

All of a sudden, however, several men friends who were in the first act come in and strangle both *Friedel* and *Minna* with gunnysacks. Then one of the men, in the course of a long speech, says the word *"schluck"* and they all go out to get a sip of something.

The third and last act seems to be laid in an attic, except that there is no roof and the walls slant outwards. On the left-hand side there is no wall at all. This gives the whole place a queer look. In come a group of men and women who apparently have just won the boat race. They murmur a great deal in their native tongue and occasionally one of them cries out something like *"bleistift."* This can't be right.

Then suddenly *Friedel* and *Minna* wander in and ask the president *"wie geht es?"* This so upsets the president that it begins to thunder and lighten and the walls fall in, killing everybody.

When the lights go on again, *Friedel* is back in the Rugs, Draperies and Linoleum Department, talking to customers. After they have been talking half an hour one of them gives a clue to what it is all about by saying, *"zusammen arbeiten."* This gives the whole thing away. The man with the red hair is undoubtedly remarking that there is only one thing that will win the day and that is "team-work."

This gives the orchestra an idea and they burst into a cadenza, at which the entire cast step up to the front of the stage and raise their arms, singing *"Du bist wie eine Blume"* as the curtain falls.

For the theatregoer who has only a few days at his disposal in Berlin we would recommend something like *"Gott Sei Dank, Der Onkel Ist Noch Nicht Wieder Zu Hause Gekommen"* ("My Wife's Uncle"). This is a comedy of the lightest sort.

The plot of "My Wife's Uncle" seems to run something like this: Breakfast is being served in the home of *Karl Geigich* and his wife *Betsy*. They argue from eight-thirty until nine-fifteen, when the first act ends.

The curtain goes up on the same scene, with *Karl* and his wife still arguing. *Karl's* face is working hard to express impatience, while *Betsy* seems to be trying to get across the idea that her old throat trouble is coming on again.

The last act shows the triumphant entry of the Emperor Diocletian into Riga. There is a great trumpeting and a man cries *"kirche!"* which, as I remember it, means either "church" or "cherry." Probably "cherry."

The Berlin season is all like that, so far as this department is concerned.

July 20, 1922

29

WAS SHYLOCK REALLY
HAMLET?

THIS department has been very remiss in the current Shakespearean discussion. Ever since Mr. John Barrymore came in with "Hamlet," followed by Mr. Warfield as *Shylock* and Miss Barrymore and Miss Cowl as *1st* and *2nd Juliet*, our contemporaries have been consumed with a fever of controversy. Letters have been written and Sunday editorials thrown off at a stupendous rate, proving that Messrs. Hopkins and Belasco do and do not know how to produce Shakespeare. Street fights have occurred between the gaffers who saw Booth and the youngsters who came of age just in time to see Barrymore. No greater proof could be had of the hold which Shakespeare has on the ages than the number of correspondents who arise at each new production and claim to be the personal representatives of the Shakespeare estate for their district.

Rather than give the impression of not being interested in this vital question, we have prepared a pretty fairly learned treatise on the matter. If you don't like it this way, you can read it backward, which is the way most of the stuff written on the subject should be read.

First comes the question of scenery. Mr. Hopkins handles it with modern (meaning Elizabethan) simplicity, Mr. Belasco with Victorian elaborateness. Both seem to us to be wrong. What Shakespeare obviously meant, especially in the coatroom scene where *Claudio* tells *Labina* to never mind, was for all the scenery to be suggested by wind currents from offstage. We are of the opinion that the entire spinning wheel scene should be played on a sort of combination veranda-cellar arrangement with no exits, or at most six, so that when *Blemio* tells *Prince Charming* of his "lawful perusals begat in testimony" it will not be so difficult for him to turn and deliver the "curly wolf" speech.

Furthermore, it is absurd to have *Flavio*, as Mr. Hopkins has him, trip as he descends the stairway before the King, as in Shakespeare's day tripping had not been taken up by the courtiers. This is proven, if our opponents had taken the trouble to look the matter up before rushing into print, by a marginal note written evidently in Shakespeare's hand, on the original manuscript of "Love's Labor Lost," which reads: "How about having *Rogerio* trip here?" and a reply, presumably from the director, saying, "Not done in court."

In the matter of textual liberties, both Mr. Hopkins and Mr. Belasco have sinned grievously. All lovers of Shakespeare will wince at the latter's heartlessness in cutting *Shylock's* "I cannot tell" speech from "I cannot tell; I make it breed as fast: But note me, signior," to "I cannot tell; I make it breed as fast." In that one cry, "But note me, signior," Shakespeare put all the venom of a despised race, to say nothing of *Portia's* love for *Bassanio* and the *Duke's* love for the little flower girl. This Mr. Belasco has wantonly thrown away.

To return to Mr. Barrymore's interpretation of *Hamlet*. Graceful, yes. Intelligent, yes, yes. But *Hamlet*, no! A thousand times no! *Hamlet* was a man-about-town. Barrymore makes him tall. *Hamlet* loved apples. Barrymore makes him sly. Those of us who knew *Hamlet* as he really was, cannot help feeling that here is sacrilege.

Now Edwin Booth, there was a *Hamlet*! We remember seeing Booth at the age of four (when we were four; Booth was naturally older) and the memory of that performance has lingered with us ever since. After it we were taken to Maillard's and had our first chicken salad. Those were the days!

Then there was Roger Meeble. Roger Meeble played *Hamlet* in Haverhill, Mass., in the fall of 1880. The week before he had played *Lord Dundreary* in "Our American Cousin" and still had some of his *Dundreary* makeup on during the "Hamlet" engagement. It was a subtly attractive *Hamlet* that he gave, one with a thousand times more fire than that of young Mr. Barrymore. To have heard Meeble read the "I will tell you why" speech was to have heard something. It was said at the time that they could hear it way over in Marblehead on a clear night.

To sum up, then.

Warfield's *Shylock* is not so good as it would have been if Warfield had played it in 1870. Barrymore's *Hamlet* is disappointing because *anybody* can go and see Barrymore, while there are only a few of us who remember Meeble. Furthermore, Barrymore makes *Hamlet* too simple. If it is going to be made so that the veriest tyro in the audience can understand the play, what is the sense in our spending our days looking up references?

And one more word, perhaps the most important, in closing. By what authority does young Barrymore inhale sharply at the end of his "What, are they children?" speech? Needless to say, there is no warrant for this in either the Quarto or the Folio. And surely, surely, Shakespeare himself never meant it. Perhaps in fact Shakespeare himself never meant anything.

January 25, 1923

EDDIE CANTOR AND "YES, WE HAVE NO BANANAS"

THE process of glorifying the American girl, which Mr. Ziegfeld undertook in his last season's Follies has hardly been accelerated by the addition of Eddie Cantor to the show, and yet the show itself has been speeded up enormously thereby. Whatever Mr. Cantor has not, he certainly has pace.

There are really two Eddie Cantors, and if you will draw your chairs up very close, we will tell you about them. First, there is the blackface comedian, who darts about like something on top of a pond, singing songs which may or may not be funny but which are always nothing for Grandma to hear at her age. For years this Eddie Cantor meant considerably less than nothing to us as entertainment.

Then last year at the Winter Garden, he washed up, and in place of the neurotic Negro appeared a Jewish boy with large, bewildered eyes and mild manner, an apologetic calm superseding the offensive assurance, and, oddly enough, a considerably more sanitary batch of songs and jokes.

Both Eddie Cantors are in the Follies this summer and you can take your choice. Ours is the Jewish boy, especially in his scene with the traffic policeman, where his eagerness to conciliate and his humility in the face of a terrific injustice borders on high tragedy.

A great many of our thinkers are disturbed at the popularity of Mr. Cantor's song, "Yes, We Have No Bananas." They see in it a sign of national disintegration. It is pointed to as one of the evil results of Prohibition or the Gulf Stream. Several leading citizens are thinking of leaving the country.

To this department it is the most encouraging lyric that has caught public fancy in our memory. In an age when we seemed sunk in a bromide mixture of spurious Mammy sentimentality and Silver Lining treacle, along comes a song which is utterly mad, almost gloriously so. And a public which had gone on for years having its opinions and enthusiasms flattened out for it in the shape of matrices before daring to accept them, suddenly leaps at this bit of flaming insanity and waves it aloft.

It is true, we were a little sorry when we found that in the verse of the song the immortal phrase, "Yes, we have no bananas," is specifically attributed to a certain fruiterer and that it arose from a confusion in learning English rather than from a native madness. But nine-tenths of the people who sing the song do not know this. To them it is simply a shouting denial of the unities of speech and thought, an espousal of a New Idea, and incidentally an easy song to sing in a crowd. A nation which will take up with a song like this is not nearly so much of a fool as it looks.

July 26, 1923

THE MARX BROTHERS

W E ARE happy to announce that the laughing apparatus of this department, long suspected of being out of date and useless, is in perfect running order and can be heard any evening at the Casino Theatre during those magnificent moments when the Marx Brothers are participating in "I'll Say She Is." Not since sin laid its heavy hand on our spirit have we laughed so loud and so offensively. And as we picked ourself out of the aisle following each convulsion, there rang through our soul the joyful paean: "Grandpa can laugh again! Grandpa can laugh again!"

"I'll Say She Is" is probably one of the worst revues ever staged, from the point of view of artistic merit and general deportment. And yet when the Marx Brothers appear, it becomes one of the best. Certainly we have never enjoyed one so thoroughly since the lamented Cohan Revues, and we will go before any court and swear that two of the four Marxes are two of the funniest men in the world.

We may be doing them a disservice by boiling over about them like this, but we can't help it if we feel it, can we? Certainly the nifties of Mr. Julius Marx will bear the most captious examination, and even if one in ten is found to be phony, the other nine are worth the slight wince involved at the bad one. It is certainly worth hearing him, as *Napoleon*, refer to the "Marseillaise" as the "Mayonnaise," if the next second he will tell *Josephine* that she is as true as a three-dollar cornet. The cornet line is one of the more rational of the assortment. Many of them are quite mad and consequently much funnier to hear but impossible to retail.

There is no wincing possible at the pantomime of Mr. Arthur Marx. It is 110-proof artistry. To watch him during the deluge of knives and forks from his coat sleeve, or in the poker game (where he wets one thumb and picks the card off with the other), or—oh, well, at any moment during the show, is to feel a glow at being alive in the same generation. We hate to be like this, for it is inevitable that we are prejudicing readers against the Marx boys by our enthusiasm, but there must be thousands of you who have seen them in vaudeville (where almost everything that is funny on our legitimate stage seems to originate) and who know that we are right.

It is too bad that with such a wealth of good material of their own our heroes should have stooped to using Walt Kuhn's "Lillies of the Field" ballet without credit. The steal is palpable and inexcusable, and all the more mysterious in view of the gigantic inventive powers of the Marxes themselves. It is as if Edison were to steal an idea for a lamp. It may turn out that the Marxes have been doing this for years, like Will Morrissey and his delightfully funny Treasurer's Report, but Mr. Kuhn certainly did it better.

One word of commendation to offset the above. In Nat Martin's jazz orchestra which enlivens the finale to "I'll Say She Is" there is no saxophone comedian. The members of the orchestra simply play the notes as written, a grateful innovation in these days when each jazz band has at least one saxophonist whose friends have evidently told him that he ought to be on the stage.

June 5, 1924

"SWEENEY TODD, THE BARBER
OF FLEET STREET"

AFTER keeping open weeks and weeks beyond closing time in the hope that the Democratic Convention would make money for them (ah-ah-ha-ha-ha-ha-ha! *make money for them*! a-ha-ha-ha!) the theatrical managers who lost their respective shirts on the venture have been rather chary about opening up any new shows. Instead of spending money in New York the delegates evidently went about picking up pennies and things that they found in the streets, so that the final score read: "New York City. . . minus $114.50. Delegates. . .$745.50." It is suggested that next year the New York *World* use its powerful influence to bring the Seven-Year Locusts to town for their gathering. They can't cost the city any more than the Democratic politicians did.

Bitten badly in this manner, the theatrical *entrepreneurs* have been crouching in their cellars, nursing their wounds and muttering. It is doubtful whether there will be any new productions now before December, and perhaps not even then. Any one wishing to see new dramatic entertainment may have to rig up something in the back yard and let the children do it for ten pins admission. The managers are nobody's fools.

Mr. Wendell Phillips Dodge, however, with the daring of the novitiate in the producing business, did take as much courage as he could cram into both hands and opened up what? A revival! A revival, mind you!

It is too early now (2 a.m.) to tell whether he was wise, or just one of those dreamer chaps. Whatever the result of his venture financially (and we will give one guess as to what it will be), he gave one poor old starving critic a pleasant evening just by raising and lowering a curtain. We were quite excited over the whole thing, got all dressed up, and presented ourself at the theatre at 7:45, applauding vigorously. The play was "Sweeney Todd. The Barber of Fleet Street, or The String of Pearls," and very well named it was, too, for it was all about

Sweeney Todd, who *was* a barber on Fleet Street in the early part of the nineteenth century and who, for a string of pearls and other goodies, committed the most fascinating and ingenious murders on his customers.

It seems, according to the criminal records of the time, that Mr. Todd had been unjustly incarcerated early in his career and had, brooding in his cell, vowed vengeance on mankind in general. On his release he set up business in a barbershop, and, as likely-looking patrons sat themselves in his chair, he would decide to "polish them off," to use his own charming phraseology, and, by a set of concealed buttons and things, would drop them, chair and all, into the cellar, where they were "polished off" and conveyed into an adjoining crypt. Here, as in the manner of a Ford truck, they went through the next stage of their metamorphosis, which was to make them into material for Mrs. Lovett's famous veal pies. The partnership of Mr. Todd and Mrs. Lovett was highly successful, until one of the pie-makings did badly in his examinations and failed to pass the test, being alive when he reached the oven department. As a result, both the Demon Barber and his sidekick were haled to court and reprimanded with the bit of rope tied tightly about the neck.

A whimsical tale, and told with considerable unction in the manner of plays of 1840, quite worth seeing if you are one of those who fall for the fallacious argument that New York is a great little summer resort.

Unfortunately, "Sweeney Todd" was not considered long enough, and "Bombastes Furioso" has been added to fill out the evening. "Bombastes Furioso" is billed as "The Oldest Musical Burlesque in the English Language," and they might have added, "the worst." We are no modernist, but anything before the nineteenth century has got to show phenomenal form to get a giggle out of us. One thing we must ask of our literary executors, and that is that none of our humorous writings be revived in 2124. Please remember this.

July 7, 1924

AN OPEN LETTER TO
THE PUBLIC

NEXT week the new season opens. (Since, for some unaccountable and probably insufficient reason, it takes two weeks to print this funny old paper, by the date of issue the preceding sentence should read: "Last week the new season opened," but we can't be bothered with the metaphysics of the thing.)

Before we start in together on our new work, you, our dear Public, and we (a work in which everyone ought to be very, very happy), there are one or two little points which will stand a bit of clarifying. This may hurt a little, but, after all, most of the things that are worthwhile hurt a little at some time or other, don't they? Or do they?. . . I wonder.

Perhaps, in the past, you have had occasion to suspect us of being not quite everything that a great, big, handsome dramatic critic ought to be. You may have felt that we were obtuse in our judgment of plays. You may have been sure that we were biased, either through money-lust or sentimental attachment, in our estimation of players. You may have thought that we were just plain stupid. (*With a shrug.*) Perhaps we have been.

But, dearest Public of them all, that is nothing to what we have suspected *you* of being. We have before us bundles of letters from you, and piles of shorthand notes jotted down after conversations with you, which we could take before any jury in the country and have two-thirds of you sent back to the seventh grade in no time. And two-thirds is letting you down easy.

In the first place, a great many people seem to take this department seriously. They read the deathless little literary *bijoux* on this page, tossed off quite obviously for the enrichment of our national letters and for no other reason, and between the lines find a tacit assumption on our part that we expect them to follow our advice in the matter of choosing plays.

"I read on your page in LIFE," writes Legion, "that 'Instep' was a good show. I spent $15 for two seats and both I and my wife decided that it was the worst thing we had ever seen. How much of that $15 did you get from the management, you dirty crook, you?"

It hardly seems necessary to point out that this is like saying: "I read on your page in LIFE that corn on the cob was a great food. We tried it the other night for dinner and it was terrible."

Several seasons ago there was a lady who felt so bitterly about our having liked "The Circle" that, just to shame her, we sent her a check for the price of her tickets. She turned the tables prettily on us by keeping, and cashing, the check. We decided that this form of sarcasm on our part would run into money if continued; so we gave it up immediately, but there is a good idea there somewhere.

If, through years of checking up on our likes and dislikes in the theatre, you find that they correspond approximately to your own, then we have no objection to your taking a chance once in a while and gambling on a couple of seats on our tip. But if, out of a clear sky, you read something on this page (which is hereby proclaimed the most unreliable, inconsistent and temperamental page of personal reactions in the country), and on the strength of it go out and pay money for a show which you do not like, and *then* write an indignant letter blaming us, we give you fair warning now that we will have you arrested.

Another small matter, before we join hands and enter new pastures together, dear Reader. There seems to be quite a bit of feeling on the part of our clients about the recurrent phrase in the Guide on the opposite page, "To be reviewed later." It is hinted that we are slacking, that we put off attending shows until it is time for them to close, that we are just a lazy Old Thing.

Now, thanks to the managers, we attend every new production on its opening night (except where two or three open together) and write the review of it that very week. But, as you will remember reading in our smashing opening paragraph, these pages are written two weeks before they appear in print, and when you see "To be reviewed later" in the Guide, it means that the play in question had not even opened at the time of—oh, what's the use in all this talk? If you haven't sense enough to have figured it out for yourself without being told, you won't understand it even when it is explained to you.

And now let's just shut our eyes and wait until next week (last week), and begin the New Year all refreshed and tolerant after this Good Talk together. . . . Only try not to be so stupid about those letters, won't you? Just remember that Mother has only one pair of hands.

July 21, 1924

THE BOY WHO GREW UP

HEAVEN knows that we are not a department to hark back to the good old days, but we must be permitted just one little lapse into that tiresome critical method because this time it means so very much to us. In the next paragraph we are going to talk about Maude Adams in "Peter Pan"; so you may skip it right now if you like.

Maude Adams came to us in "Peter Pan" at just the age when we were ready for a great emotional upheaval. At fifteen one is first beginning to realize that everything isn't money and power in this world, and is casting about for joys which do not turn to dross in one's hands. Miss Adams made us cry for the first time since our final spanking, some three years before. That, you must admit, is quite an event in a young man's life. We were on the road to Damascus, and near the corner of Broadway and Fortieth Street, in the Empire Theatre, when we suddenly saw a great light and changed our name from Saul to Paul, becoming the beautiful character that you see us today.

In view of this (which we hesitate even to talk about in print) we may perhaps be excused from anything more than a formal statement that an *espèce de* "Peter Pan" is now being presented at the Knickerbocker Theatre, with Marilyn Miller heading the cast.

On second thought, we have decided to get a little sore about it. Very sore, in fact. Because this production of "Peter Pan" represents something in the commercial theatre of today which is so terribly wrong that there is little hope for anything so long as it persists. We refer to a complete and abysmal ignorance on the part of a majority of the theatrical *entrepreneurs*, an ignorance of the meaning of the plays they produce, an ignorance of the spirit which motivated their writing, and an ignorance of the public for whom they are supposed to be presented.

The fact that a script like that of "Peter Pan" could fall into the hands of people who didn't know last January that Marilyn Miller could never be *Peter Pan*, beautiful and graceful as she is, any more than Mary Eaton or Julia Sanderson or seven hundred other beautiful and graceful ladies could ever be *Peter Pan*, shows exactly what is wrong with the commercial theatre today and what will probably be wrong with it tomorrow. The fact that people should be allowed to present this play who would interpolate a Broadway song hit into it, shows exactly what is wrong with the world.

That song hit was particularly revolting. It was bad enough when *Peter* sang it to *Wendy* as they sat by the fireplace, a tawdry affair on the order of "Look for the Silver Lining," about Home being the best little thing after all. But all through this, and all through the rest of the disheartening performance, we sat waiting for the final curtain, where *Peter* stands among the fireflies in the treetops waving goodbye, because we didn't see how they could spoil that. This scene might, we hoped, recapture something of the original charm.

And when it finally came, and the curtain started descending on that memorable picture, what happened? The orchestra began plugging the song hit just as they do at the final curtain of a musical comedy, and to the strains of this Tin Pan Alley whistler, the most fireproof asbestos that we have ever seen came slowly down on our shattered temple.

"Shattered temple" because, most unforgivable of everything, Mr. Basil Dean and the rest of them made us see that "Peter Pan" isn't really so splendid after all. Even had some one more suitable than Miss Miller played the rôle, we doubt whether we could have kept our illusions about it. It is just plain dull in great, long stretches. It is even worse in others. Aside from the moment when little Miss Carol Chase, as *Liza*, drawing herself up to her full three feet, said "Pooh!" with such force and artistic fire as to throw herself completely off her balance, we got scarcely a thrill from the words Barrie had written.

Perhaps the fault was not entirely Miss Miller's, or Barrie's, or Mr. Basil Dean's. The trouble probably lay in our having once been fifteen and, being fifteen, having seen Maude Adams.

November 27, 1924

43

TWO WAYS

G IVEN: An old husband, a young wife, a virile and contiguous young man. This triangle has long been the basis for one of the four great national jokes of France. In Russia they make tragedies out of it.

In America we do both. The subject has been taken by Eugene O'Neill and tortured into a terrific catastrophe with the title "Desire Under the Elms." Sidney Howard has fashioned a fine comedy from the same material and called it "They Knew What They Wanted." We rather think that, on the whole, Mr. Howard has done the better job, for his comedy has moments of great pathos, a necessary thing for comedy, but Mr. O'Neill's tragedy has moments of unconscious comedy, a terrible thing for a tragedy.

"Desire Under the Elms" is, up to a certain point, one of the finest things O'Neill has ever written. It shuts down over you with its cold damp, until, in spite of the eight different varieties of New England dialect (all wrong but one) which its characters speak, you feel that you are a part of the rocky farm on which the scene is laid and that you are never going to get in even to Boylston Center again.

Then something happens, and Mr. O'Neill goes quite mad. It is almost as if he were burlesquing his own tragedy. Like Hardy, who, frenzied with the taste of heart's blood, has two-thirds of his characters in "The Return of the Native" commit suicide by jumping into a brook one after the other, O'Neill takes his people and has them wallow in *Weltschmerz* until the chief protagonist can think of nothing more terrible to do than threaten to turn all the cows loose. Unless the cows should enter into the spirit of the thing and tear moaning down the road, this would seem a rather flat manifestation of tragedy. One pictures them rather as stopping a few feet away from the barn and wondering meditatively what it was all about.

With his sudden access of energy, the author becomes positively phony in his theatrical repetition of catch lines and "significant" situations, and what was earlier in the evening a grand play ends in a blaze of green fire with an imaginary orchestra playing "The Funeral March of a Marionette."

Mary Morris and Walter Huston, especially Miss Morris, are worthy of the first half of the play, than which we can think of no higher praise.

Mr. Howard, on the other hand, has dared much more than Mr. O'Neill in running this theme through a comedy. There are times when you don't see for the life of you how the thing can possibly end tolerably. Yet it does, and with a great deal of distinction, too. With several scenes of industrial sociology deleted, it will be one of the few fine American things that the Theatre Guild has done.

Of course, Pauline Lord raises it to heights which make even the qualification "American" unnecessary. Her *Anna Christie* was undergraduate work for *Amy* in this play It is just about as near a perfect performance as you are likely to see. Glenn Anders, in spite of the fact that on the opening night he was not allowed to take a curtain call (or at any rate *didn't* take it), contributed the next most satisfying characterization and, in every way, held up his end of the remarkable scenes with Miss Lord. This does not mean that Richard Bennett did not practically tear our hearts out, but he is one of the stars and everyone knows that he is good. Mr. Anders if very young and has had to live down "The Demi-Virgin," and so his splendid performance seems a much more important piece of news. All in all, it was a big night at the Garrick.

December 11, 1924

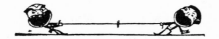

LABOR TROUBLES

T HIS department has had considerable trouble in the past with its circus-reviewing staff. One year we sent our seven-year-old son to cover the event, and, while his reporting and judgment were satisfactory, he became intolerable in the consciousness of his success and at the sight of his opinions in print, and demanded a raise in wage (from fifty to seventy-five cents *and* taxi fare to Madison Square Garden).

So the next year we employed scab labor in the person of our five-year-old son, who was only too willing to do it for a quarter and pay his own taxi fare out of that. But he was unreliable as a reporter, owing to its being his first circus. The thing ended in his bursting into tears at the explosion of the clown automobile (a thing this department feels like doing to this day) and having to be led out. The resulting report, as it appeared on this page, was incoherent, to put it charitably.

This year, then, being still of the belief that the circus should be reviewed by a minor, we decided to spend money like water and send both boys, now aged nine and six respectively. In this way we hoped to get the mature opinions and cool sophistication of one in combination with the enthusiastic though temperamental reactions of the other, and between these perhaps some fairly definite idea of what the circus is like. That is just what we did not get. The two reports are contradictory in practically every respect and are worthless. Such as they are, we print them below, with apologies to those readers who are accustomed to rely on this page for its news of the world of entertainment.

On the circus program we find a note to the effect that "During the progress of the menage number, Alf Loyal's Miniature EQUI-CANINE CIRCUS will make its first American appearance on one of the stages."

According to our elder reporter, the "Equi-Canine Circus" consists of a troupe of little black dogs with false heads on to represent horses. The younger reporter insists with considerable heat that they are *real* little horses. Anyone who says that they aren't, is crazy—and something of a cad. In the first place, they *look* like real horses and in the second place, they *are* real horses. His senior asks, in a cynical manner, if he ever heard of horses as small as that, to which the answer is no, but you don't have to have heard of a thing to have it so. The rest of the argument is not important enough to be put into the record.

Another feature of the circus which made a great impression on the nine-year-old is the loss of a bustle by a clown who is dressed as a woman. According to this report, the clown is walking around the ring when suddenly the bustle, together with half of the skirt, comes off and stands stationary while the rest of the clown goes ahead. On his attention being called to it, he turns and whistles, whereupon the bustle in the skirt starts running toward him and joins itself to its proper place. It is all very, very funny.

The junior member denies that this happened at all. It is merely a figment of his brother's imagination. What really occurred was that a man came running by with a skeleton chasing him. The man screamed but the skeleton stuck close, and they both disappeared through an exit. There was absolutely nothing about a woman with a bustle.

And so it goes. One says the real feature of the show is a man who sits on a big tower of tables and gradually tips over until they all fall with a crash. The other admits that this was all right in its way, if you like that sort of thing, but maintains that the real artistic event of the afternoon was a man who came in and allowed another man to blow him up by means of a tube inserted under his waistband to a size never before attained by any man in the history of the world.

The general effect of these reports is so confusing that it will be necessary for this department to visit the circus in person to see just what really goes on.

One thing that the young critics did not experience at this performance in Madison Square Garden was a queer feeling around the diaphragm at the thought that this is the last time the blare of the band and the crack of the whip will ring out through the spaces of the big barn. For before another spring comes around the Garden will be torn down. We would devote a sentimental paragraph here to the ghost army of clowns, prizefighters, prize Airedales, prancing horses and motor boats which might well attend the last night of the building's career, but last year we wrote a similar paragraph against the threatened destruction of the Hippodrome, and the Hippodrome is still standing and packing them in. When we see with our own eyes the gaping hole in Madison Square where the Garden once stood, we'll do a really fine paragraph. We're nobody's fool.

April 16, 1925

A NOTABLE REVIVAL

O N THIS, the third birthday of "Abie's Irish Rose," it is only fitting that all levity should be dropped and that, in honor of its 1292nd performance in New York, breaking the world's record and the heart of this department, we should discuss the thing seriously from the standpoint of dramatic history. There has been too much fooling about it. It is a serious matter.

Let us consider "Abie's Irish Rose" as it will be considered in English courses two hundred years from now, or by dramatic critics of 2125 when it is revived, with all the old-fashioned costumes and scenery, by some highbrow producing organization devoted to resuscitating twentieth-century plays.

"Abie's Irish Rose," probably the outstanding play of the twentieth century that we have any record of, was written by Anne Nichols, and first produced in New York (according to the old playbills) on May 22, 1922, at the old Fulton Theatre. Professor Barnder Methews, in his "Anne Nichols: Her Life and Times," says that the author tried unsuccessfully for many months to sell her play to the obtuse managers of the day, and was finally forced to produce it herself, with the result that she made some three hundred and eleven million dollars (about six million reefs in our modern money) and bought the entire harbor of New York. The play ran for eight consecutive years in New York City and then was subsidized as a permanent exhibit by the city in an outdoor theatre in Central Park, along with the Zoölogical Reservation. It also played in every city in the country, and in towns where there were no theatres it was given in private barns. This should be proof enough that at no time in the history of the theatre up to this point had the spirit and imagination of the people been so stirred as it was by this play. It was, in effect, the beginning of the Second Renaissance.

A brief summary of the plot of "Abie's Irish Rose" will serve to show its delightful reflection of the twentieth- century spirit in the United States and, even today, its wit sparkles with the freshness which will not be denied.

Solomon Levy has a son, *Abraham*, a typical twentieth-century boy. The father is afraid that the boy will marry someone not of the Jewish faith. The son has, as the play opens, just secretly married an Irish girl by the name of *Rosemary Murphy*. He brings her home to meet his father, but, on confronting the old gentleman, loses his nerve and introduces her as his affianced bride, "Rosie Murpheski." The old man is naturally very much pleased that his son has chosen a Jewish girl, and plans for the wedding to go ahead at a delightful rate. There is, running through the play, a comedy character, a little man named *Isaac Cohen*, who is thought by some commentators to have been a satiric thrust at Chief Justice William H. Taft, a noted jurist of that time.

On the day of the wedding, the bride's father, *Patrick Murphy*, arrives in company with a Catholic priest, *Father Whalen*, to witness what he thinks is going to be the wedding of his daughter to an Irish boy. The meeting of the two fathers, Jewish and Irish, just as the knot has been tied, is highly comic and flashes with American wit. "You'll be goin' where it's so hot the thermometer won't register," says one irate parent, to which the other replies: "I'll keep it that way for your arrival!"

As a result of the ill feeling over the deception, the young folks are cut off from their families and go to live for a year by themselves in comparative poverty but great happiness. On Christmas Eve a reconciliation is effected, however, and the Jewish father and Irish father are brought together on finding out that, not only has there been a baby born to bear an Irish name, but there have been *twins*, permitting the perpetuation of the Jewish name as well. The curtain falls on Jew and Irish, priest and rabbi, *Abie* and his *Irish Rose*, all very, very happy. Underneath the sparkle of its dialogue, the play carries a lesson for each of us today, the lesson of religious tolerance.

Technically, the play is a perfect example of twentieth-century playwrighting. Fast moving, dynamic, closely knit, it marches to its conclusion with the remorseless inevitability of Greek tragedy. Its periods are well sustained, and the conflicts and peaks skillfully handled. Nichols knew her theatre. She knew her public. She knew her human nature. In "Abie's Irish Rose" she has given the ages a comedy that stands by itself, and the theatre-going public may well thank the Windowpane Players for reviving it.

May 21, 1925

49

PARIS LETTER

FORTUNATELY for the readers of this department, your correspondent was in time to see the gala three-thousandth performance of that French masterpiece, "*La Rose Hibernaise d'Abie*," now in its sixth year at the *Théâtre République*. (Readers who translate French readily are requested not to give away the secret to those who might otherwise be mystified.)

The complete Gallic flavor of this comedy is as rich now, in spite of its long run, as it was on the day when the author, Mlle. Anne Nichols, presented it to M. Olivier Morosque for production, and, by the time it has completed its tenth year at the *République*, it will be even richer. These French, these French!

For those who have not already read the plot of the piece as published in *Le Journal Menorah* or (*ou*) *Le Temps de Kilkenny*, a brief *résumé* may not be out of place. We translate literally, and with considerable pleasure:

M. *Cohen*, a metropolitan *tailleur*, has a son, *Abie*, who gives him no end of trouble because of his random amours. As the scene opens a succession of young ladies knock on the door to demand overhead charges from the old man, promised them by the son in his various expansive moments. *Cohen père* is at his wits' end. He tears at his hair and shouts "*Oi, Oi!*", which is an old Savoyard phrase meaning: "What is it that I shall do, please?"

At this point *Cohen fils* enters with *Rose*, his latest encumbrance, whom he introduces to his father as the mother of an old schoolfriend. The old man asks how it can be that a girl as young as *Rose* could be the mother of a boy as old as *Abie*, and the son explains that it is on account of the difference in exchange rates and the low value of the franc. This the old gentleman believes and makes advances to *Rose* as soon as *Abie* has gone out to pay the cabman.

In the meantime M. *Murphe*, an elderly *contractant* who has been paying for *Rose's* singing lessons, has discovered her absence, and comes rushing into the room demanding that she return to him. Discovering her with *M. Cohen*, he accuses her of infidelity, at which she laughs bitterly. The son returns, and the three men proceed to scratch one another.

Abie, to placate his father and reassure *M. Murphe*, promises not to marry *Rose*, and the young couple depart for Trouville, leaving the two old gentlemen excellent friends over a bottle of *anis deloso*.

It will be seen from this that *"La Rose Hibernaise d' Abie"* is a typical product of the French theatre, out of the soil of France, and representative of the spirit which resents debt-refunding to the last sou. The cast, which has remained intact during the long run of the play, is as follows: *Isaac Cohen*, M. Deschamps; *Patrick Murphe*, M. Duval; *Isador Levy*, M. Pecheux; *Mrs. Cohen*, Mlle. Hyacinthe; *Mrs. Levy*, Mlle. Renouardt; *Father Whalen*, M. Barouille; *Rabbi Samuels*, M. Desvalières.

It is hoped that Mr. Otto H. Kahn can be prevailed upon to bring the entire company to America in the fall to present *"La Rose Hibernaise d' Abie"* before a New York audience.

We hereby promise our readers that this is the last time we shall use "Abie's Irish Rose" as material for this page, and that, with the resumption of local items in the new season which opens in August, we shall abstain from both this source and contemplation of the droll doings and sayings of Monsig. David Belasco. It will come hard for us at first, as we have built up our entire répertoire on these two unfailing friends, but somehow, somewhere, we have heard a notice saying: "Lay off," and we are not the department to run a thing more than a kilometre into the ground.

Of course, the ideal solution would be for "Abie's Irish Rose" to stop running and for Mr. Belasco really to retire and throw away his sailor-suit collar, but until these daydreams come true, we really have other things that we must attend to.

June 25, 1925

51

MUNICH LETTER

F OR A really amusing review of a German play, the reviewer should not know the language at all. This will enable him to make funny guesses about what is happening on the stage, and the whole thing will make no sense at all.

If there was one qualification, then, that we had for reviewing a German play, it was a complete misunderstanding of German. We can bring eight or ten instructors to New York within a week who will swear to it. One of the most beneficial results of the war was that it relieved us of the necessity of apologizing for our German.

Confident, therefore, that we would be in total ignorance of the proceedings, the best bet seemed to be something called "Woyzeck." It was billed as a "tragedy in twenty-three pictures." Could anything be more promising material for a funny paper than a German tragedy in twenty-three pictures? We had to laugh just to think of it.

"Woyzeck" turned out to be a complete flop as comedy. In the first place, they all spoke so slowly and distinctly that we could understand almost everything that was said. We tried not to. We even made believe that we hadn't, and jotted down comic remarks on the program. But even at that, the acting was so effective that we couldn't squeeze out even a giggle, and even wept a bit at times.

The play, which is by Georg Büchner, would delight the hearts and the audiences of the Provincetown Players. Twenty-three pictures showing the gradual disintegration of the soul of a stupid private under the mass attack of his superior officers, a psychoanalyst, and his woman. An understanding of any language at all, and you can understand "Woyzeck." With the exception of one scene, it stands ready for New York production. We recommend it to any theatre south of Fourteenth Street.

Note: Having just discovered Herr Büchner and mentally classified him as an ultramodern, we find that he has been dead many years and that "Woyzeck" is an old German favorite. What must you think of us?

Better luck attended our visit to Sudermann's "*Stein Unter Steinen.*" We didn't understand more than a third of it, owing to the bad German spoken by the entire cast. Only one of them spoke Harvard German at all, and that was in a scene by himself.

The thing seemed to revolve around a poor man with a blond beard (German theatrical beards are infinitely superior to those in London), and we gathered that he had done something terrible. He worked in a stone-cutter's place and no one would have anything to do with him. They all said "*Na, na*" to him, instead of "*Nein, nein.*" He was awfully unhappy and had quite a lot to say about the Human Soul and what a rotten time it has. In spite of this, however, he did manage to escape being hit by a big stone block which the villain dropped near him. It doesn't seem probable that, the play being by Sudermann, there would be a happy ending, but really, that's the only way we could figure it out. At any rate, he threw a kiss to the girl as the curtain came down and was smiling for the first time in the performance. Perhaps there was another act that we didn't stay for.

If we were to write down our reactions to the operetta, "*Schwarzwaldmädel,*" you would call us "Old Softy." But there was something about the dingy, 1897 poverty of the old Gärtnerplatz Theatre, with its sparsely-filled pit and crowded galleries, its musty atmosphere of down-at-the-heel bravado and its heavy-footed heroines and rich-voiced heroes singing, with all the happiness in the world, the "one-two-three, one-two-three" Schwarzwald melodies, that seemed a sadder aftermath of the war than anything in Paris. If only the theatre had been more up-to-date or the music less gay.

August 6, 1925

VIENNA LETTER

Vienna, July 19th

WE HAVEN'T very much money left, but we would gladly give fifteen or twenty dollars of it (a little over a million kronen in vanilla money) to watch George Bernard Shaw's face at a performance of his "St. Joan" such as is being given here by the Russians of Tairoff's *Kammertheater*. If he is the man that he ought to be, he would laugh his head off.

For these Russian boys have taken his sacred script, which the New York Theatre Guild nearly bled itself to death over, and have put it on with boards and gunnysack and made a circus of it. The characters, with the exception of *Joan*, are clowns. The settings are thrown together out of ill-fitting laths. The *Dauphin*, in actual clown makeup, with a little hat on the side of his head and a long feather trailing to one side, sits on an arrangement of boards like the bleachers at the Polo Grounds, clad in skin tights with a tiny dab of imperial ermine on the shoulders, and giggles pleasantly while huge, bulbous-nosed churchmen discuss the state of the realm. The soldiers wear flannel uniforms, with nominal tin fittings to suggest armor, and tomato-can helmets. The *Maid* alone is immune from the devastating parody.

All this, of course, sharpens the satire to the point of burlesque and makes it a hundred times more malign. If Shaw really means to kid his countrymen, if the centuries and centuries of repetition of the same old historic formulas, the pomp and ceremony and the majestic clash of arms, are to him the bunk that they seem to be, than he ought to adopt these Russians as his sons. If he is sore at what they have done, he doesn't understand his Shaw, that's all.

After "The Miracle," we rather felt that Max Reinhardt had some working arrangement with God, whereby he was to handle all terrestrial productions on a flat ten per cent. basis and see that they were done right. This contract is off, if we have any influence at all. For at Reinhardt's own *Theater in der Josephstadt*, under his own direction, we have seen as ham a performance of *"Jaurez und Maximilian"* as you could find outside the Grand Opera House, Boston. There is stamping and raging and eye-snapping, and a last-minute hope of reprieve from the Governor, together with considerable mutterings under the breath. All in all, something for thirty-five cents.

The fact that the play itself is nothing but an old-time historical bass drum, such as has put the Eaves Costume Company on its feet, doesn't help the Reinhardt case much. With one or two exceptions, the acting and direction are as ham as the script. The Russians, with their ramshackle production, the down-at-the-heel Germans in their dingy theatres in Munich, almost any organization of actors who read the newspapers at all, could do better by the beautiful theatre in which the Reinhardt organization is housed.

The settings are, of course, effective, but not one whit (one whit equals two jots, four jots one tittle) more so than what Jones, Simonson or Geddes could do with one hand and four fingers behind the back. Tomorrow night they are going to do Galsworthy's *"Loyalties,"* and if they charge through that as they did through *"Jaurez und Maximilian,* Mr. Galsworthy will have grounds for legal action. If the thing really was, as the program states, *"unter der Führung von Max Reinhardt,"* the Beechwood Players of Scarborough, New York, should be greatly encouraged. They have done better under these very eyes.

A charming little bijou called *"Oscar mit der langen Nase"* at the *Kammerspiele* only goes to prove that the double bed is an international prop, that you don't have to understand German to get around in Vienna, and that Avery Hopwood has nowhere near exhausted his supply of foreign adaptations.

The discouraging part of our Vienna campaign is that we had to come all the way to Austria to enjoy Russian players, when, for much less money, we could have stayed right in New York City, their home grounds.

August 20, 1925

BUDAPEST LETTER

Budapest, July 26th
(that would be about eight cents in American money).

J UST at present, there are more Hungarian plays in New York than there are
in Budapest. The big show here is *"Charley nénje,"* or, as we used to call it,
"Charley's Aunt." The chief item of interest connected with *"Charley nénje"* is
that the role of *Stephen Spittigue*, who is—take it from the program—a genuine
"oxfordi ügyvéd," is played by Z. Molnár L. You will recognize Molnár as an old
New York name. Tóth Böske is also in the cast.

When names mean as little as they do in Budapest, the best way for the
theatregoer is just to drop in at something he sees open and take a chance. You
have your choice of *"A nota vége,"* *"A kék madar,"* *"Nyari kabaré"* (this is at the
Vigszinhaz, in case you lose your way and have to ask), *"Régi jo Budapest!"* (that
last word means "Budapest," the name of the town), or, if you are just tired and
want relaxation, *"Az Apolló-Szinház vendégjátéka."* So you see, it doesn't make
much difference what you choose. You can't win.

As the program contains the names and casts of every play in town (evidently
some local Shuberts control the whole system), there is no way of telling the name
of the play you are witnessing. It gives you something to do during the performance, to check up and see if you can guess.

In the one we saw the first night, a man came in very excitedly and said to his
wife (it *must* have been his wife) that *"munkatarsaimnak pedig hodolat es hala!"* She
just laughed at this, as well she might. Infuriated, he hung up his hat and began to
eat. Then the landlord, or perhaps the train conductor, came through and
evidently threw a bombshell into the household by saying that he was somebody's brother (*sombodig broder*). This was enough to end the first act. (We had
arrived late.) The second act we saw in another theatre.

There was music in this act. In fact, the whole thing turned out to be a musical
comedy. There is one good thing about musical comedies: they are the same in

56

every country. Without knowing a word of Hungarian, we knew exactly what was going on, because we had seen it going on in American musical comedy ever since we were a tiny, tiny boy.

The scene was, as usual, in a modiste's shop, with people passing by on the sidewalk against the backdrop. Every third one would enter the shop, flirt with one of the girls, find that his wife was in the next room trying on a gown, and then sing a song. The funny man was the porter and was in love with the French maid. He sat on a hatbox with her and sang a song about "*mindenekelott szotlan*," which meant that he had some idea of finding a cozy nook beside some babbling brook and building a little bungalow for just me and you (*jostv meg a jo*). Then the girls came in and laughed heartily in Hungarian and there was a finale.

Having had enough gaiety, we ended the evening at a play in which no one character had any connection with any of the others. They all went right ahead and seemed to be trying to see who could finish first. The doctor's wife went to the window and let in a little fellow, who went to the cupboard and took out a general. The general was an exceedingly likeable man who went right off and never appeared again. This gave a girl in white a chance to say something to a friend of hers who was downstairs and all seven of them began writing. Just before the curtain came down, it turned out that he was really the son of the mill-owner and that he had been posing as a postman only to see if she really loved him for himself and not for his money. We couldn't find the name of the author on the program, but we think it was Ring Lardner.

August 27, 1925

ANNOUNCING DEFEAT

THE moment of high tragedy in a critic's life comes when, sitting idly at the play, he feels the first flush of hardening of the arteries creeping over him. The only honorable thing for him then to do is to rip the epaulettes from his shoulders and turn in his sword in the Quartermaster's Department. But we, having already sensed the ominous *retour d'âge*, still linger in the ranks, craven that we are. God help us, we have no other trade.

The first chill came over us early this season and has been increasing in intensity nightly, until we know now what manifestation our collapse will take. We are no longer able to sit through a musical comedy.

For ten seasons we have smiled at people who have said, "I don't see how you stand it, going to the theatre every night. Don't you get awfully fed up?" and have replied: "Youth, my dear Countess, youth, which suffers long and is kind, keeps us fresh and tolerant, and no show, no matter how bad, can combat our love for the theatre." And then we would seize the Countess and dance a rigadoon.

But with the coming of the season 1926-27 came the touch of the Icy Hand. We first detected it at "Queen High." Now "Queen High" is an excellent musical comedy. It has one of our favorite comediennes, Luella Gear, and two funny men—Frank McIntyre and Charles Ruggles. It has a highly tuneful score by Lewis Gensler and a book based on "A Pair of Sixes," which in its day was a popular farce. There is nice dancing and food for the most captious eye. And yet, as we sat there admitting to ourself that it was a good show, we had a feeling that we probably would not like the next one we saw, or the next, or the next.

This presentiment was so accurate as to be positively uncanny, for the next one we saw was "Naughty Riquette." The score for this is by Oscar Straus; so it probably is good. The star is Mitzi, and while we have never proposed marriage to her, we have usually been able to abide her antics. And there is a really comic clown named Stanley Lupino, at whom, in the old days, we would have laughed outright. But at the sound of the familiar choruses and the sight of the early Madge Lessing formations, we felt the congealing process coming on and when finally Mitzi sprang the big gag of the show, which is to call a bothersome matron a "popeyed old pelican," we turned completely to stone.

Nothing happened at "Castles in the Air" to relieve our atrophy. This opus comes from Chicago with the ringing of bells and huzzas of the multitude, and probably has many good points. We hold no brief for our attitude. It is our misfortune. But here again we were thrown into a state bordering on death by the cries of "Here comes the Prince!", the red-coated military, and the susceptible peasantry who run on and off screaming and laughing just as peasantry has been running on and off screaming and laughing to our certain knowledge for thirty years. The chorus work is skillful and Vivienne Segal sings well, while Bernard Granville does everything that we could expect with the comedy. But to no avail so far as we were concerned.

The final proof of our insensibility came at "Countess Maritza" and "The Ramblers." In "Countess Maritza" we found the highly praised Kalman Viennese score, the elaborate production, the effective clowning of George Hassell and even the graceful dancing of Carl Randall something less than interesting. And now that we have collapsed, we may as well admit that we have *always* been bored stiff at these superior musical shows from overseas, beginning, if you must know, with "The Merry Widow." Nice music, yes. But much nicer when played by itself.

It broke our heart to find ourself unmoved at "The Ramblers." As one of the early devotees of Bobby Clark in his burlesque days, we have always laughed at his shooting cigar and animated cane and especially at his coy sideways glance at the culmination of a particularly raucous gag. But this year we sat and waited for him to pull something new, and, when it did not come (we except the very funny farewell chorus in the middle of the second act), we even resented the roars of laughter with which his old stuff was greeted. "The Ramblers" is a much better and funnier show than the average (it would have to be with Kalmar and Ruby at the typewriter), but it came to us in our Dark Hour, and through it we know that we are licked. From now on a younger and a fresher man must cover musical shows for us.

October 7, 1926

THISTLES FROM A
THISTLE BUSH

W E ARE usually quite prepared to be proven wrong in our opinions, because we usually *are* wrong, but in the matter of the dramatization of Dreiser's "An American Tragedy" all the expert testimony in the world cannot shake us from our belief that it is a heavy-handed, obvious, badly done play. Just the kind of play, in fact, that the novel deserved.

Mr. Kearney had a tough job to make a drama out of those two volumes jammed full of stereotype, newspaper clippings and old cigar wrappers. Dreiser got his effects through sheer tonnage. Mr. Kearney had to let people go home at the end of two and a half hours. The fact that he sends some of them home crying after his hero has been led off to the electric chair is no credit to him or to the acting. People are going to cry when a young boy is led off to be killed, no matter if the scene is tacked on the end of "Charley's Aunt." Anybody can make people cry that way, so long as he doesn't dress his hero up in a kilt and redden his nose. And even then you will get quite a bit of sniffling.

Here is a play without one line of distinction, one touch of subtlety, one bit of acting which is anything more than adequate, and, in the last ten minutes, by utilizing a trick as old and as sure-fire as dispossessing Grandpa and Grandma from their cottage, crawling under the tape in the guise of a powerful drama of human emotions. We could get pretty sore thinking about it. In fact, we are.

Just as in the book Dreiser took no chances on his readers' ever having read a book before, making it incumbent on him to wave a red lantern four blocks before a character acted and a green one four blocks after, so in the play we find the boys and girls signaling the gradual approach of their emotions in plenty of time for you to slip out and have a smoke before their fruition. In fact, you could spend most of your time in the smoking-room and still have a pretty good idea of how things were working out upstairs.

For example, Morgan Farley—who is about as suited for the rôle of the baffled bellhop as the young John Keats would have been—has a big scene on a couch (all the big scenes are played on couches, accompanied by sufficient heavy breathing to sail a small boat clear across Central Park pond) in which he is inspired by a newspaper story to drown *Roberta*. To most adults in the audience the birth of the evil idea is evident at once. But Mr. Farley, lest there should be some mistake, is forced to carry on a remarkable dialogue with himself, with illustrated slides showing the workings of his mind, until the wonder is that the victim herself didn't hear him and take the next train for Canada.

The same grammar school tactics are followed throughout, from the very first scene to the one where *Clyde*, immediately on being convicted by the jury, rises from his seat and dictates a telegram to his mother, specifying everything except whether it is to be sent as a straight wire or a night letter.

Dreiser has been called our pioneer modernist and doubtless the play, because of an explicit seduction scene and a clinical conference with an abortionist, will be classified as highly modern realism. But all the sexual interpolations in the world cannot alter Dreiser's kinship to Horatio Alger or remove the play from the category of old-fashioned hit-and-run dramaturgy. Horatio Alger and "Frank the Young Naturalist" have always had a wide appeal, and probably always will, but let us have no more to-do about their or "An American Tragedy's" being Great Stuff.

On the other hand, we cannot share the ennui with which some of the reviewers sat through the Theatre Guild's presentation of Werfel's "Juarez and Maximilian." We did not see this on the opening night and the performance is said to have profited greatly by certain destructive criticisms that were made. But, later in the week, it seemed to us to be a highly effective and moving account of the historic failure of one man to combine Christianity with empire-building. It may have been the 1865 frock coat, but we were conscious throughout, in the sensitive performance of Mr. Lunt, of the presence of a futile and inexperienced Lincoln.

Devoted followers of this page, by turning to their files for 1925, will discover that we were not crazy about "*Jaurez und Maximilian*" when we saw it in Reinhardt's Theatre in Der Josephstadt in Vienna. It may have been that our Harvard German wasn't up to the occasion, but we are also sure that the Guild company, with Alfred Lunt, Clare Eames, Arnold Daly, Edward G. Robinson and

Margalo Gillmore, did much better by it than the Max Reinhardt stock company. And the next time the Salzburg Sage comes to America, he might well take a look at Lee Simonson's settings.

November 4, 1926

JUST A TOUCH OF HERESY

LIKE "Iolanthe's" *Strephon*, this department is ambiglandular. It is Gilbert-and-Sullivan from the waist up (which, unless we are all wrong, includes the heart) and rebel from the waist down. We should be entirely Gilbert-and- Sullivan were it not for the Gilbert-and-Sullivan fans.

We defy any one to enjoy the Savoy operas more than we do, and yet when all the faithful get together at a performance of one of them and demand encore after encore, beating their palms together to the evident discomposure of the cast who have no more verses to sing, and when they laugh loudly over and over again at the same joke, and when they hum the score over with the orchestra during the overture and nod knowingly in advance of all the gags, we are ready to take up with Con Conrad and Anne Caldwell and depart, dignified and stately. (So self-conscious have these zealots made us that we refuse even to put quotation marks around "dignified and stately.")

All of which is to apologize for any excess of enthusiasm we may show in saying that Mr. Ames' production of "The Pirates of Penzance" is swell. It has its faults, just as Messrs. Gilbert and Sullivan had their faults. (Just a minute, please, while we step aside to dodge the falling heavens which will be along any minute now following that last remark.)

Chief among the faults of the production (really the only fault) we would specify the attempt to pad out the action with leapings and boundings and rollings on the floor. Even if it could be proved to us that they were a part of the original direction, we should still maintain that there is too much of them. One feels like saying, as one says to a child along about five o'clock on Christmas afternoon, "That isn't funny any more." In fact, if someone had said that very thing to Mr. Gilbert once or twice there might not be the occasional momentary confusion in the lay-mind as to whether it is "Iolanthe" or "The Pirates" that is being done.

But we have already subjected ourself to enough masochistic torture in writing the above. The whole thing is just grand, including the Woodman Thompson settings and costumes and the new voice (new to the Ames stock company) of Miss Ruth Thomas, whose rendition of "Poor Wandering One" was almost enough to make us forsake our ferocious allegiance to "Thou the stream and I the willow" in "Iolanthe."

But there we are, talking like a Gilbert and Sullivan pest again. All we ask is to be allowed to enjoy "The Pirates" in our own way, which is with a swelling bosom and brimming eye, but practically no noise.

If, by the time this comes out, the Theatre Guild has gone through with its rather unscientific scheme of taking "Ned McCobb's Daughter" off at the end of three weeks to make room for "The Silver Cord," resuming it again at the end of another three weeks, those who rely on this page for their spiritual guidance will have to wait until January tenth before seeing it. Our advice would be to set aside some day during that week for that very purpose, for it is an excellent piece of work and fine entertainment.

In it, Sidney Howard has combined his experience in the theatre with his experience among the natives of the State of Maine, and the result is quite the best thing he has done. Which, considering "They Knew What They Wanted" and "Lucky Sam McCarver," is saying quite a good deal.

The event is made even more satisfactory by two sterling performances in the leading rôles, Clare Eames appearing as the Superwoman of the Kennebec and Alfred Lunt as the Superman bootlegger. The conflict between these two people of "character" assumes titanic proportions and the decision is in doubt up to the final bell. When you consider that last month Miss Eames was the *Empress Carlotta* and Mr. Lunt the *Emperor Maximilian* (and very imperial they were, too), it seems extraordinary that they could shift with such conviction into a Maine housewife and a South Boston bootlegger. Mr. Lunt's metamorphosis, with the gold tooth and all, is positively creepy. And his performance magnificent.

December 23, 1926

ADD FOLK PLAYS

T HE past few weeks have belonged to the amateur rather than to the professional in what, for lack of a longer term, we will call Our National Theatre.

Broadway may have been dark, but our schools and colleges have been a-buzz with exclamations of parental pride mingled with the murmuring of the prompter, as the actors and actresses of the Little Theatre of Tomorrow creaked back and forth across the temporary stages and made believe they were somebody else.

These performances have ranged in ambition from outdoor Greek drama (at times a bit hurried in tempo because of the rumbled threat of a shower in the offing) to class-reunion shows "worked up" late in the afternoon before the performance. Of the two, the latter type is easier to watch.

In these informal productions there is less strain on the actors, whose only concern is to keep upright and *on* the stage. And, as in any theatrical performance, professional or otherwise, the less strain there is on the actors, the easier it is for the audience.

Although these strange folk plays performed at class reunions appear in no manuscript form to speak of, a transcript of the proceedings (taken down by a broad-minded male stenographer) might read, in part, as follows:

ACT 2

(Act 1 having been omitted owing to the non-appearance of five of the principals. These appear somewhat later and insist on giving their act on the veranda while Act 2 is still in progress. Their audience is recruited in large blocs from the main auditorium.)

Entrance of a fair proportion of the cast, in reunion costume, with some attempt at rhythmic movement to the tune of "Hallelujah"! The lyric, as picked out by watching the lips of the more capable singers, seems to be:

"Hallelu-jah! Hallelu-jah! Here we are, Big 1912.

(*Repeat*)

"Nobody something something something,

"But you can't something, something, something,

"Hallelu-jah! Hallelu-jah! Here we are, Big 1912!"

Apparent end of song, although several die-hards continue for another line or two, amid thunderous applause. A conference of principals is then held and it is decided to give in to the popular demand and sing the whole number again, with repeats. At the conclusion of this, in spite of vociferous demands from sections of the audience for more, the dialogue is launched:

1st CITIZEN: Well, well, what ever became of George Wisser?

VOICE FROM AUDIENCE: Yeah! Wisser!

2nd VOICE FROM AUDIENCE: He went to Princeton!

ENTIRE AUDIENCE: Yeah—Princeton!

1st CITIZEN (*addressing audience personally*): He couldn't go to Princeton, he didn't have a signet ring. (*Entirely extemporaneous line but very popular.*)

2nd CITIZEN (*with some idea of getting along with the show*): Well, Eddie, what *did* become of George Wisser?

GEORGE WISSER (from audience): Here I am! Fast asleep!

(*At this, pandemonium breaks loose, and, encouraged by cries of "We want Wisser!", Mr. Wisser climbs up on the stage and joins the cast.*)

3rd CITIZEN: Why, hello, George! Want to be in the show?

GEORGE WISSER (*Suddenly disgusted with the whole thing*): No! (*Climbs down and goes back to his seat.*)

At this point someone, dressed for no reason at all to represent President Lowell of Harvard, arises and announces that there will now be a song by Arthur Welson entitled: "If I Send My Son to the Dental School, Will a Gold-Digger Teach the Class?" This is met by a storm of disapproval, and Arthur Welson is never heard, chiefly because of cries of "Louder!"

At this point the entire entertainment is taken over by the audience for a period of about ten minutes. Sex or seven members climb up on the stage and three or four of the cast visit with cronies in the audience. "Hallelujah!" is sung several times and one or two announcements are made, preceded by much banging for order. Finally, one of the class marshals makes himself heard to the following extent:

CLASS MARSHAL: Come on now, fellows! Tony and the rest have worked hard on this show and are trying to do something for the class. The least we can do is to sit still and be quiet. Everybody back in his seat, now!

There is general cheering at this and several of the more earnest classmates take their seats. The rest mill about at random. In the meantime, the show has been begun again, starting with the entrance of the chorus singing "Hallelujah!"

This goes on for some time.

CURTAIN

July 7, 1927

THE DRAMA IN VIENNA

Vienna, July 16th

T HE theatrical season in Vienna suffered a temporary setback last night, owing to the fact that all the actors and audiences were hiding in cellars. You can't put on much of a show with everyone under hogsheads six or seven blocks away.

It seems that someone (thought to be the Shuberts) started a revolution just at theatre-time, and you know what a revolution is. Gunfire, gunfire—gunfire.

At the *Ostbahnhofschauspielhaus* the *Ostbahnhofschauspielhausgesellschaft* was playing a piece of Von Reitergenossen's called *"Die Passionsblume"* when the shooting started. The first act opens with *Niegratz* reading a letter from *Ulma Lufdorf* in which she says that she doesn't see any reason why they can't get together on this thing and show a little cooperation. She asks him if *Gelba* is standing in his way. Just then a servant comes in and says that there is a man named *Janssen* who wants to see *Niegratz*.

Janssen enters and the two men sit down at the table and order *Paprikahuhn mit Nockerl. Janssen* then draws out a map on which he points out where the new clubhouse is going to be if they can ever raise the money. While they are talking *Irma* enters and starts flirting with *Niegratz*. He takes her in his arms and they sing a duet called *"Es ist gleichgültig ob es gebilligt wird oder nicht."* It was at the third bar of the second verse of this song that the revolution started outside in the Ringstrasse.

Just as *Niegratz* sang *"Es ist gleichgültig ob—"* a large bullet came through the door from the alley and fixed the glass chandelier just dandy. Another came through the back- drop and skimmed over the *Paprikahuhn*. The actor playing the rôle of *Janssen* was found this morning in Burgdorf, a suburb of Vienna, under a clothes hamper. *Niegratz* and *Irma* went up the aisle and out into the lobby, where, after looking at their billing and assuring themselves that their pictures were in

68

the frames, they left for Czechoslovakia. The performance was called off for the duration of the war.

The report was the same from other theatres in Vienna, indicating a general slump in business throughout the city. Some managers blamed the weather, some the unseasonable gunfire, but the consensus seemed to be that something would have to be done to get the actors and audiences out from under the beds before the box offices would begin to pick up.

August 11, 1927

ALL ABOUT
"STRANGE INTERLUDE"

W E MIGHT as well get this out of the way right at the start: Eugene O'Neill's "Strange Interlude" is a highly important play, probably a great one, and one which is bound to mark a turning point of one sort or another in dramatic history.

Personally, as one who sat constantly interested from 5:15 in the afternoon until 11 at night, with an hour's recess for dinner, we were at first irritated to the bursting point by the pretentious banality of the lines, then gradually caught up by the sweep of the thing until, in Act 6, we were completely under its spell, and finally—Mr. O'Neill having gone burlesque, as is his custom of late toward the end of his plays —thrown back into a state for which "irritation" would be too strong a name. The total impression on us was that something big and fine had been slightly muffed—maybe by Mr. O'Neill, maybe by us.

Our irritation arose from the method which the author has chosen to use in writing his drama—a pompous resuscitation of the old-fashioned "aside". The reason that the play takes so long is that each character, in addition to speaking his lines, must also speak his thoughts. This would not be so bad if their thoughts were worth speaking, but, for the most part, they could easily have been guessed by any alert child in the audience. In certain scenes, notably the one in Act 6 where the woman sits with her trinity of complementary male units, all thinking out loud, this method justifies itself and gives a hint of its possibilities in the future.

But throughout most of the play, especially during the first acts, when soliloquy seems simply a lazy man's method of writing exposition (and essentially false as well, for no one thinks expository thoughts—unless perhaps he is waking up after a hard night and is trying to satisfy himself as to just who he is and whose house he is in), Mr. O'Neill's "asides" are scarcely distinguishable from those of the old-fashioned melodrama, and are certainly not much more subtle. When *Darrell* enters and *Nina* says aloud to herself (*Darrell* conveniently waiting until she is through thinking): "My old lover. . .how well and young he looks. . .now we no longer love each other at all. . ." there is more than a passing similarity to the speech of *Richard Rackmorton* in "The Wolves of St. Agnes," where he steps to the foots and says behind his hand: "I wonder if she suspects that I am really her father. I will test her," and then, turning to *Dora* (with slightly more bass in his tone): "Little girl, do you remember the swans in the lake at Passy where you used to play?"

There are few of these "asides" of O'Neill's which any good actor or actress could not indicate without speaking a word or any good playwright get into his lines without resorting to tricks. Some day this method will be used by an author whose characters don't act as they think and who also has the gift of humor. That will be something different.

There is a certain effect of having lived the lives of the characters in "Strange Interlude" when you finally emerge into Fifty-eighth Street which is likely to be confused with having believed in them. This is simply because you have been cooped up with them so long. You can read one of Dreiser's novels— or rather, *if* you can, you get the same effect, just from continued proximity. We used to feel that we knew the characters in James Fenimore Cooper's novels, not because we liked them but because the English Department made us finish them. Any playwright who can make his audience stick with him for five hours has an advantage over his rivals. He can impress them by sheer tonnage.

Evidently no author except O'Neill can make an audience stick for five hours. If Samuel Shipman had written the first act of "Strange Interlude" (and he could have), the play would have been laughed off the stage. If Mae West had written the boat race scene in Act 8 (and she wouldn't have), every reviewer in town would have taken the day off to kid it. It is natural that O'Neill should command respectful attention because he is our foremost playwright. It is natural that "Strange Interlude" should hold people in their seats, first, because of its intrinsic interest and ambitious scope and, second (and no less important), because of the fine performance of Lynn Fontanne, together with those of Earle Larimore, Glenn Anders and Tom Powers. No cast ever had a tougher job.

But since O'Neill *is* our foremost playwright, and since the pretensions of "Strange Interlude" *are* so great, it is only natural that we should expect it to be practically perfect. And it isn't—not by a million miles.

February 16, 1928

IN THE VERNACULAR

SOME day (it may be any day now, just as soon as the frost gets out of the ground) we are going to write an exhaustive treatise on the subject of slang.

For instance, "Whispering Friends." A good, frank discussion of "Whispering Friends" ought to bring the subject of slang down to, say, 1910—or whatever year was given over exclusively to the use of the word "skidoo." We are not sure that "skidoo" was actually used in the course of the play, but there were moments, as we sat listening to Mr. Cohan's reminiscent dialogue, when we felt the years slipping off us and we found ourself back at the little old red schoolhouse, wondering what chorus girls were really like, and crying softly to ourself at the thought of the little boy Benchley who might have been. He was such a fine, manly chap—that little Benchley—with his golden curls and his cute way of cocking his head on one side whenever he wanted another of Grandma's cookies. And then had come long trousers and his first waltz, and sex had raised its ugly head—Heigho. We rubbed our eyes and the play was over and we found ourself back in 1928, with its jazz and its tall buildings, and no one to remember the good old days of "23, you big piece of cheese." No one, except Mr. George M. Cohan.

Not that Mr. Cohan's latest work is entirely bad, either. In spite of some of the dullest dialogue that we have heard in many a day, he has managed, by virtue of his knowledge of what we Broadwayites call "good theatre" (the opposite to this is "bad theatre"), to keep an extremely artificial situation fairly interesting for perhaps an act and a quarter. But in matters of comedy we have been led to expect, from him at least, something besides smooth direction, excellent casting and clever juggling of a thin plot, and when we say that the lines in "Whispering Friends" aren't very funny we don't want any arguments about the fact that the audience seemed to be laughing their heads off. That was what they tried to tell us about that play—what was the name?—the one about a Jewish boy who wanted to marry an Irish girl, or maybe it was an Irish boy who wanted to marry a Jewish girl—anyway, there was a rabbi and a priest in it, and you know what happened to *that* play. So let Mr. Cohan take warning and not be deceived by those laughs in the audience. They don't mean a thing.

Continuing our subject of—what was it? "slang"—well, continuing our subject of "slang," we come to "The Bachelor Father," and here we find an interesting example of what is known as "Onderdonk's Disease." Onderdonk was an English playwright (1794-1911) who was afflicted with a curious malady which took the form of a desire to write a play about Americans. Never having been to America, he did the next best thing and subscribed to *Punch* for a year, at the end of which time he had a very good idea of how Americans really talked.

Now the curious thing about "The Bachelor Father" is that the author, Mr. Edward Childs Carpenter, is an American himself, and yet he seems, somehow, to have contracted a slight touch of the old Onderdonk trouble—possibly from rubbing against an Englishman in the subway or somewhere. At any rate, it is a mild case and is only really noticeable in the first act, when June Walker, as a Hogan's Alley "mick," is forced to carry on one of those "hully gee" conversations, so full of "wisecracks" (none of which got even a snicker from the audience) that we were just reaching for our hat when Geoffrey Kerr sauntered on and in his always delightful way restored the conversation to a nice, quiet normalcy. And from then on, the play was pretty thoroughly enjoyable.

It wasn't Miss Walker's fault at all, that bad start, and once she was relieved of the strain of working into her conversation all the American humdingers from 1911 to 1928 (not inclusive), she settled down to giving one of the most attractive and appealing characterizations of her career. As the American representative in the internationally illegitimate family of Sir Basil Winterton, V.C., K.C.B., K.C.G.M. (played superbly by C. Aubrey Smith), she wins her way into her delighted and immoral father's heart and into the heart of her audience, which, judging from the tongue-clicking around us, was equally delighted but slightly more moral. Nor did the female acting honors go entirely to Miss Walker, for a young lady named Adriana Dori aided the play immensely by being exactly what the author intended for her part—that of Miss Walker's Italian and equally illegitimate sister, with aspirations for grand opera. Miss Dori can act, and she can sing—an unusual combination of gifts which saved Mr. Belasco and the audience a great deal of trouble and suspense. Rex O'Malley, in the rôle of "third bastard," was also quite good and we would only recommend that he practice just a little bit longer with his left hand—you know, that passage where it goes C-sharp, F-sharp A and then that quick trill with the second and third fingers. It would help immensely that illusion of him as a gifted young pianist.

March 22, 1928

JUNIOR DRAMA

Latitude 41.54 N.

Longitude 58.27 W.

THE dramatic season on the French Line opened this afternoon at three sharp with a performance in the *Guignol,* or, as you Americans say, the "Punch and Judy." It was held in the Children's Room and was a gala affair, except for one little girl who was badly frightened and had to be led out. She was much too young to have been brought, anyway, and it is to be hoped that the *Guignol* season will not receive a black eye around the ship because of this one small critic who left early.

The French give themselves much more latitude in their Punch and Judy (as they do in so many other of life's pleasures) and do not feel obliged to stick to the old plot every time. In fact, *Punch* and *Judy* as characters did not appear on the opening bill at all. The only familiar touch was the hanging at the end, doubtless put in as a concession to public sentimentality.

The bill consisted of two pieces—one a curtain raiser called *"La bonne Chance de M. Mouton,"* and the other a realistic crime melodrama entitled *"Le Voleur"* (not the Bernstein piece recently revived by Alice Brady). Both plays were strictly original and dealt with two of the more sordid phases of life in Paris. One might almost object to them on the ground that, while such low characters undoubtedly do exist in real life, they are not what one goes to the theatre to see. However, this department has never been one to cavil at the theme of a play and we do not intend to begin caviling now, at least not in mid-ocean.

The first piece, *"La bonne Chance de M. Mouton,"* hardly calls for extended comment. It was received with marked indifference by the first afternoon audience, as it deserved to be. What seemed like hours of expository dialogue between *M. Mouton* and a character who appeared to be a Chinaman of some sort thoroughly bored the spectators and there was a great deal of fidgeting among the younger members of the audience (those between three and four) and practically a running fire of high treble conversation with nurses and parents. It was not until *M. Mouton* (played with little or no distinction by the largest puppet of the troupe) began beating his wife that the audience showed signs of following the plot at all.

This sudden sadistic streak in *M. Mouton* came as quite a surprise, as he had seemed entirely devoted to dialectics up to this point, besides being a man well along in his seventies. But evidently *Mme. Mouton* was a type which irritated him, for he beat her into insensibility and threw her out behind the house for no particular reason. We are sorry to report that this brutality pleased the audience enormously, and that there were loud demands for more.

In *"Le Voleur"* (in free translation, "The Thief") we find more of that gaiety which one associates with the French, although here, too, we should say that the French puppets hit each other much harder than is necessary and display a viciousness in belaboring a victim after he is obviously unconscious which detracts a little from the light-heartedness of the comedy.

The plot of *"Le Voleur"* is soon told—if at all. A lady keeps placing articles of furniture out on the sidewalk in front of her house (either the reason for this is not brought out in the dialogue or our French is not what it was), only to have each article in succession stolen by a mean-looking man as soon as she goes back into the house for more. A piano, a table, a dish-cabinet, and finally a bed are thus taken right under her very eyes, and a gendarme who is called in each time proves to be worse than useless, owing to drink. The whole thing up to this point is very improbable, but it drew down screams of laughter from the audience and so justifies itself on the ground of being what the public wants.

The thief is finally apprehended through trickery (we were asked not to divulge the plot), and is beaten in good old French fashion until his head hangs limp over the edge of the stage-apron, after which he is given a couple more socks for good measure. Then, to make doubly sure that he will menace society no longer, he is hanged from a gallows and the magistrate and gendarme dance away with him in a coffin singing *"Auprès de ma Blonde."*

We have gone into this plot at length because it seems to indicate a tendency on the part of the French to follow the Eugene O'Neill influence in cumulative tragedy. Not one piece of furniture is stolen, but four, each one larger than the last. Not one sock on the nose is given, but eight. The protagonist of the drama is not only killed by beating—he is hanged as well. It is Life closing in on him. It is Truth and Beauty.

Incidentally, we should like to complain of just one thing in the Children's Room equipment. The chairs are awfully low for a six-foot spectator, and tip over too easily when the ship rolls.

March 29, 1928

HORREUR!

FOR THOSE of our little readers who are accustomed to wallowing in gore each year at the Grand Guignol we have bad news. The Grand Guignol has gone nance. With the new bill (we were present at the opening night, which, in Paris, is about as exciting as being at the opening of a Waldorf Lunch) the direction has changed hands and the new management seems to have a distinct aversion to blood.

According to the program, there will be no change in policy. You will get your chills and nausea just the same under the new régime as under the old. But if we are to take the new bill as an earnest, the horrors are to be more mental, with less of the tearing of flesh and grinding of bones which made the old Grand Guignol so homelike and cozy.

The big number on the new Grand Guignol program is called *"Les Nuits du Bagne,"* which is plenty horrible but with practically no loss of blood. The *bagne*, as you probably know (as we didn't), is not a bath, but that peachy old prison where bad French boys are put for the rest of their lives to more or less disintegrate. The *nuits* which are held in the *bagne* are something to write to your Congressman about. It seems that the headmaster of the *bagne* comes around with a thumbscrew every night and applies it to those who haven't finished their number-work, and naturally the boys dislike him. One of them, who seems to have had the measles or some other prison complaint which has practically eliminated his eyes, finally gets back at the headmaster by putting his head in a brand-new device just imported into the prison for a better disciplining of the prisoners. The effect is much the same as if he had killed him.

So you see, it is not the old Grand Guignol at all, but the product of a newer and softer civilization. When we think back on *"Le Crime dans la Maison de Fou,"* in which the two old crazy women—but there, we are getting sentimental!

We will say this for the Grand Guignol, however, The company which presents these little bits of horror, with now and then some little bits of comedy, is one of the best crews of actors we have ever seen. If they were not, much that is now horrible would be just ridiculous. Their French is so clear and well spoken that even your correspondent had little difficulty in following (which reduces it practically to an argument over my aunt's inkwell and the apples, pears and walnuts which are in the dish), and the acting itself is something which many of our Broadway boys and girls could watch and watch and watch and still not be able to beat.

And this from one who has never before had any feeling for French plays, French acting or French food. *Zut!*

Not to wax fulsome in our new-found enthusiasm, may we say that *"Vient de Paraître"* (or, as our publisher is so fond of saying, "Just Published") is another example of what easy, affable acting can do for a moderately amusing comedy. The play, by the way, is by the author of "The Captive," who seems to have adjusted himself to the more conventional modes of fun-making. It might be something for Roland Young if translated into English, although the excitement in America over the winning of a literary prize would hardly justify putting on a comedy with that as its base.

We hope that we are not going to be one of those who are constantly seeing chances for effective translation in foreign plays. If you catch us at it, please write in and stop us. But (to revert to the Grand Guignol for a minute) if some of our boy-actors want a swell little sketch for vaudeville, written in the best Booth Tarkington manner, they could do no better than get in touch with someone about *"Le Haricot Vert,"* which was on the Grand Guignol bill before the present one. It may be just a teenty-weenty bit risqué (we weren't quite sure about one or two of the words), but it seemed one of the nicest bits of juvenile comedy since "Seventeen."

There—now we've been constructive!

May 10, 1928

TRYOUTS

BETWEEN the closing of one theatrical season and the opening of the next ("comes a pause in the day's occupations that is known as the Children's Hour") several hundred plays are "tried out" in the provinces to see what they need before being brought into New York. It is usually found that they need amputation just below *and* just above the knee. Not enough of them, however, are thrown into the incinerator after the tryout. The managements of many of them seem to have some ingenuous idea that they can be "fixed" and that they will then knock the metropolis cold. "The third act needs a little rewriting," they say hopefully, "and we need someone else as the parson, but aside from that we're set." And there is another drama lined up for us slaves of the public to write an obituary for.

Avid, as usual, for news, this department has been spending these hot summer weeks going about the Atlantic seaboard spying on abortive dramatic entertainments in the outlying districts, with an eye (sometimes one eye, sometimes two) for possible metropolitan material in the fall. And we must admit that, so far as we have seen, nothing is fit to come into New York at all.

Take, for example, the show put on for the benefit of the Yacht Club at Sinosset, Rhode Island. It was called "The Sinosset Follies of 1928," a title implying that there have been others like it in years past and are likely to be more in the future. Reason totters at the very thought of such a sequence. We have laws against liquor and smallpox. Are the "Sinosset Follies" going to be allowed to run their course year after year? It were better that the Sinosset Yacht Club fell into decay like the castles of the Rhineland than that such a thing should be perpetuated.

The opening chorus of "The Sinosset Follies" consisted of six young men and six young ladies in yachting costume (or what passes in Sinosset as yachting costume). The lyric to this chorus was written by J. Foster Wrenn, Chairman of the

Entertainment Committee and a perfect peach of a chap who, had Fate not made him an indifferent architect, would most certainly have given both the Gershwin brothers a run for their money. All the lyrics in the show, you will find, were written by J. Foster Wrenn, and based on existing lyrics by Lorenz Hart and Buddy De Sylva. Mr. Wrenn also coached the show and worked awfully, awfully hard to make it a success, and everybody ought to be awfully grateful to him—or else take a good sock at him.

The opening chorus is followed (after a short wait while the backdrop is disentangled from the borders) by a sketch showing one of the less attractive phases of social life in Sinosset, intelligible only to very old Sinossetites and not very pleasing even to them. The author of the sketch is not mentioned, and the supposition is that the actors are making it up as they go along.. Then comes a number in which a young lady and young gentleman sing and, what is even worse, dance to, "You Took Advantage of Me," for which they can be prosecuted and sent to jail by the management of "Present Arms!" now running in New York. And if the management of "Present Arms!" have any social conscience at all they will hire Clarence Darrow and spend millions on the prosecution. This department will head a subscription list with $100 right now.

When "The Sinosset Follies of 1928" breaks up at a quarter before one in the morning, its patrons have been treated to three paraphrases of current popular songs, two very long monologues (one of which was fortunately cut short in the middle by the monologist's falling off the platform and disappearing for good), a finale to the first part, a finaletto, a grand finale to the whole show involving fourteen more people than the stage would hold, and four comedy sketches based on topical Sinosset situations which were not essentially dramatic in themselves and which, even had they been excerpts from "The Wild Duck," would have lacked a certain something as entertainment. These were interspersed with rather long announcements by J. Foster Wrenn in person, who, in common with three or four thousand amateur announcers throughout the country, had seen M. Balieff on his first appearance in this country and had been known as the local "Balieff" ever since for no discernible reason. This epidemic of amateur Balieffs is one of the major harms done this country by the introduction of the Chauve-Souris eight years ago.

As it was rumored backstage that a representative of Ziegfeld and one of the Shuberts in person were out front looking for possible metropolitan material, all of the actors were in great form and doing their best, which, unfortunately, was not quite good enough.

We have singled out "The Sinosset Follies of 1928" because it is representative of a type of entertainment which is going on all summer from Maine to—what is the name of that state?— California, but other productions which we have seen in our tour of inspection have just as little chance of getting into New York in the fall. Among them we may list the revival of "Pinafore" given, much to the disgust of Messrs. Gilbert and Sullivan, by the summer colony at Eagle Lake, Michigan; a kermess entitled, "Around the World with the Roses," which had the ostensible excuse of providing recreation for the indigent pets of Santa Ira, California; and, as bad as any of them, a performance of "Within the Law" given by a summer stock company composed of "guest stars" from Broadway who were taking their vacations by not learning their lines for a new show each week.

The fact that the Drama survives the body blows given it by amateur and professional organizations each summer should be proof enough that it is an essential feature of our civilization. It *should* be proof enough, but, for us, it isn't.

July 26, 1928

NEW RESOLUTIONS

EXT week, if you will ask "Mummie" to let you sit up very, very late on the evening of August 23, you may be able to get one of the early editions of this magazine in which will be found our first review of the New Season (1928-29). Of course by then the New Season will have been bowling along for about two weeks, but it does not become a *de facto* season until this department has accorded it official recognition. That is the Law.

You may think it all very fine and thrilling to have so much power and prestige that a whole great, big dramatic season stands waiting for one department to say "Yes" or "No," or perhaps "What time is it?" but the responsibilities of such a position are very heavy. We may actually have to return to New York and *see* some of the new plays.

According to the advance dope-sheet, the first entries are to be "Elmer Gantry," something called "Trapped," and the "Vanities of 1928," Mr. Earl Carroll's first venture since his graduation. Writing this, as we are, about a week before they have opened, and with no necktie on, we have a hunch that "Elmer Gantry" is going to be one of those early-season novel-dramatizations which, along about November, will be recalled only by those in the profession; that Mr. Carroll, fortified by the costly presence of W.C. Fields and a couple of Dooleys, will come across with a good one; and that "Trapped" will be one of those Max Marcin melodramas. This eerie prophecy on our part will probably send the ticket agencies out scurrying to buy eight weeks ahead on "Elmer Gantry" and to dump their holdings in the "Vanities." Such is the power of the Press.

But, whatever turn the new season takes, this department is going to be a much better boy, beginning with next week's issue. We are going to make this just the best and most inspiring dramatic page in the whole school and are going to do everything in our power to win the Edyth Totten Prize for the neatest manuscript written on the subject of "What I Did on My Vacation." You will be surprised at how much better this department is going to be from now on, provided you can find it. It will always be about four blocks over from the Will Rogers campaign matter and just before you get to the Ornithological News.

In the first place, we are going to see every play that comes along, even if it is produced by Gustav Blum. No matter if it is going to close the next night, or even if it closes while we are there, we are going to see it and write about it.

Our reason for this resolution is not to make the page more comprehensive but to irritate ourself. We have been getting a little soft of late and need to be aroused into an ugly mood. We have been concentrating on the plays that we could be nice about and passing the others over with a brave little laugh and a toss of the head. From now on we will see all and say all, and will probably get a good push in the face before October is over. But our readers will have known the truth.

Sooner or later in the life of a dramatic reviewer comes the problem of whether he is to write for that large majority of his readers who know nothing about Show Business or for those who are in the profession. Copy which makes good reading for one class is deadly dull to the other. In reviewing a play for the trade one must mention minor members of the cast, like a community newspaper's account of local theatricals: "Also very good were Clarence G. Deefish as *Lord Gotrocks*, Lillian Menderson as the maid *Beeper*, Theodore F. Fonsgerk as *Policeman* and Roger Flann as *A Mess of Pickerel*. Jervis W. Lastic made the part of *Thorton* a very real character and Blanche Omshell kept the audience in gales of laughter by her antics as the *Archbishop of Canterbury*."

Now such accounts are all very well for those readers who know Theodore Fonsgerk and Lillian Menderson but to the vast unenlightened majority they are so much type, and we have, in common with the presidential candidates, decided to cast our lot with the vast unenlightened majority who know about Ethel Barrymore and Ed Wynn and let it go at that. In other words, this page will contain breezy, badly spelled essays on subjects suggested by current plays, with just enough news interspersed to make them dull, and will interest only those members of the theatrical profession who like *belles lettres* or who want to be thrown into a rage. Our friends in the profession (of whom there are now seven as opposed to twelve last year) need expect no favors of us, unless perhaps they can see their way clear to sending us a hundred Melachrinos at Christmas time.

So you see, this page is really going to be just about the same as it has been for the past eight years, except for a vicious note which will come as the result of our being unable to drink anything with our dinner. Our motto will be, "One for all and all for fun, and tea for two and two for three, and one for the little boy who lives in the lane." On this platform we shall stand or fall. Take it or leave it.

August 16, 1928

HARPO, GROUCHO, CHICO, ZEPPO AND KARL

I F WE were one, or all four, of the Marx Brothers we should be a little confused by the judgments passed on us by the two visiting British journalists now on the staff of the N. Y. *World*. Mr. St. John Ervine, exercising his unquestioned prerogatives as the guest of a free country, was not pleased with the new Marx show, "Animal Crackers." On the other hand, his countryman and colleague, Mr. William Bolitho, was so impressed by it that he wrote an appreciation in the same journal which must have thrown Die Gebrüder Marx into a panic of apprehension. We are afraid that from neither critic did they derive much practical help in their work.

Mr. Ervine had probably heard too much about how funny the Marx Brothers were, a fatal preparation for any critical viewing. Someone might have told him, however, that Zeppo Marx is not *supposed* to be funny and thus have saved him from being so upset by the discovery when he made it. It must be difficult, in dealing with so strange a tongue as American, to tell right offhand whether an actor is supposed to be funny or not. We may also perhaps attribute a little of Mr. Ervine's coolness in the face of Groucho Marx's barrage of wisecracks to a certain unfamiliarity with the words used. For, from Mr. Ervine's own genial attempts to be colloquial in the vulgate, we are quite sure that he couldn't have understood more than a third of Groucho's highly modern references. Chico Marx, in spite of having the answers in one of the most devastatingly mad scenes in modern drama, left Mr. Ervine neither one way nor another, and it was only Harpo, who speaks the universal language of pantomime (and lechery), who registered with the visiting commentator. All in all, pretty nearly a wasted evening for Mr. Ervine.

But even Mr. Ervine's disapproval must have been more comprehensible to the Marx family than Mr. Bolitho's enthusiasm, for the latter understood them better than they probably understand themselves. As so often happens these days among earnest critics, deep and significant symbolisms were read into this harlequinade which, if generally accepted, would lower clowning to the level of a Channing Pollock morality drama. Harpo is, to Mr. Bolitho, "the simplest member to understand," and yet he is a "suppressed wish-complex." We wonder, or rather Mr. Bolitho wonders, "at the inviolable mutism he keeps proper to his extrahumanity, at his phantom tricks which belong to a largely incommunicable dream world." Harpo should know about this.

"Groucho," says Mr. Bolitho (and he may be right), "is at the same time less elemental and more complicated." We learn that he is the sublimation of the Jews' attitude toward life, "the exteriorization of this faithful power of laughing at themselves." The group, as a familiy, may possibly "immortalize themselves and become stock characters as enduring as the angel and the devil of the Talmudic legend." Of the two British opinions, we think we would rather have Mr. Ervine's condemnation. At least, he can plead ignorance of what it was all about.

The Marx Brothers ought to be very easy to enjoy. We find it absurdly simple. In the first place, we know the language, which is a great help, and, in the second place, we don't stop to think whether we are laughing at Harpo's inviolable mutism or because he is just comical. When Groucho says to Chico: "You look like Emanuel Ravelli," and Chico says: "I *am* Emanuel Ravelli," and Groucho retorts: "No wonder you look like him. But I will insist there is a resemblance," we detect no symbolism of an oppressed Jewry, but rather a magnificently disordered mind which has come into its own. And in Chico's suggestion that, in order to see if the stolen painting is perhaps hidden in the house next door they first *build* the house next door, we can find nothing which would qualify the brothers for participation in a Talmudic legend, but rather something which makes them a frantically transitory comet formation which we can proudly tell our grandchildren of having seen one night in 1928. For we doubt that the Marx Brothers have any successors.

November 16, 1928

TURNABOUT

EVER since the disbanding of the old Charlot troupe several years ago, the incomparable Beatrice Lillie has been saddled with Anne Caldwell librettos of various kinds and has been forced to sit more or less idly by and watch her ex-teammate, Miss Gertrude Lawrence (also incomparable in her own field), flutter past in the golden hits of Messrs. Aarons and Freedley. It is now Miss Lillie's turn to laugh coyly from over her fan, for Noel Coward has provided her with "This Year of Grace," a layout after her own (and the public's) heart, while Miss Lawrence finds herself in the awkward position of carrying a very wet albatross by the name of "Treasure Girl."

Noel Coward has proved himself nothing short of a wonder man in the concoction of "This Year of Grace," for which he has written the book, music and lyrics, besides taking part in it himself. It is the kind of revue that one might dream of writing for a completely civilized world and, so long as people crowd in to see it as they are doing now, we are prepared to retract everything we have ever said against Mankind. If Mankind wishes, we will even indorse it—blindfolded. But unless someone in America is able to do something that approximates Mr. Coward's feat, we shall always feel that it was a mistake to break away from England back there in 1775.

After years of reciting Miss Caldwell's and other natives' lines it must seem like heaven to Miss Lillie to find herself back in the "bus rush," or singing "Britannia Rules the Waves" in the world's low-water mark in bathing suits, or executing a gorgeous burlesque of Miss Lawrence herself in "I Can't Think." To sing quietly through a number like "World Weary," confident that one of the biggest laughs in the theatre is waiting at the finish, must be a very comfortable feeling. And, incidentally, Miss Lillie sings the quiet part of this song well enough almost to get by with it as a straight number, for, as a result possibly of her chastening experience with American-made books, she has acquired a calm, almost a sadness, which does much to enhance her comedy. Since the first Charlot revue so many local young ladies have taken to using her intonations and gestures in private conversation that she does well to leave the more obvious of them to her imitators.

Perhaps we have already indicated that we hold Mr. Coward's talents in high esteem. We have not, however, mentioned the finesse of his own personal performance in such recitations as the outline of the plot of the ballet, "The Legend OF the Lily OF the Valley," or the singing of his own macabre number, "Dance, Little Lady," which latter vivid attack on society is probably in for frequent and clumsy imitation in future revues.

We should like to point out, however (and God help us for mentioning good English to an Englishman), that the meticulous, though quite natural, pronunciation of the word "dance" on the part of the chorus only accentuates the slight irregularity of such a sentence as "Teach Me to Dahnce Like Grandma Dahnced." If one is going to pronounce it "dahnce" (as one very probably should pronounce it), one should also say "*as* Grandma dahnced." It fits in a little better with careful usage.

However, the only credit which America can take in the whole remarkable evening's entertainment is the sensational waltzing of Moss and Fontana—and they probably came originally from somewhere else.

Probably Miss Lawrence's "Treasure Girl" isn't much worse than the average carriage-trade musical comedy. It just seemed so, on the night following "This Year of Grace." Certainly Mr. Gershwin's score contains some excellent numbers, but somehow they sound to better advantage when played on the piano at home.

(*Time out for momentary inquiry into why most musical comedy numbers sound better when played on the piano at home.*) Our theory is that, unless the orchestration is especially good —which it isn't in this case—the messing about with the tempo which has to go on in a show in order to give the singers time to do their stuff spoils whatever swing and individuality a tune may have. This accounts for your finding out later, when you hear it played for dancing, that it is a much better tune than you thought at the show. One or two of the numbers in "Treasure Girl" are among Mr. Gershwin's best, but you would never know it. Mr. Ira Gershwin's lyrics are, as usual, unobtrusively excellent.

The drag on "Treasure Girl" comes in the story of the treasure hunt which somehow keeps Walter Catlett, Clifton Webb, Mary Hay and Paul Frawley, not to mention Miss Lawrence, constantly moving about in a feverish attempt to make something out of nothing. We still feel that the lines aren't any worse than in most shows of this kind—certainly they are better than those in "Three Cheers"—but they obtrude themselves more and seem worse, and there is a general atmosphere of a lost cause about the whole thing which depresses the cast as well as the audience. It is only when Miss Lawrence starts to dance, or Bobby Connolly's superhuman young ladies come tearing on, that life seems to start in the old bones and perceptible fluttering of the eyelids is noticeable.

Miss Lawrence is, of course, Miss Lawrence (except when she tries to be someone else) and, so long as this is true, "Treasure Girl" will probably attract that large section of the theatre-going public for whom just watching Miss Lawrence is enough pleasure for one evening. (Our license number in this group is 1,497.)

But while Miss Lawrence is not on it would be well if Mr. Catlett were given a new gag or two, Miss Hay and Mr. Webb another routine, and Miss Gertrude McDonald taken out of hiding and allowed to dance by herself. It would also help if they could manage to find the treasure early in the first act.

November 30, 1928

OLD WINE

A PLAGUE of revivals usually descends when the theatres are empty of other attractions, but this season, cockeyed to the last, has brought forth a whole week of them right in the middle of its busiest activity in other lines. It would serve them right if we passed over them entirely for bothering us when we had so much else to think of, but it so happens that one or two of the revivals are better than most of the new shows on the list.

"The Wild Duck," for example. It is unfair to look for anything as good as "The Wild Duck" in any season, for the chances are that it won't be written. We do not intend to make this department any more ridiculous than it already is by praising this play of Ibsen's with the fervor of a pioneer. Everyone who has ever seen "The Wild Duck" must have gone away with a bruise between the eyes where it hit him. It is the only play we have ever seen, or expect to see, where Comedy and Tragedy are fused into the same moment, where we laugh at *Ekdal* as he sits at the table compromising with his coffee and, at the same time, dread to hear the sound from the imitation hunting preserve outside which will mean that little *Hedvig* has taken the expert's advice and shot "against the grain of the feathers." That fifth act of "The Wild Duck" is an act in a million (and we have seen only a few thousand acts) and, on seeing it for the third time the other evening, we again had to be asked to leave.

The Actors' Theatre is the organization which has given it to us in revival, as it did several years ago, and Blanche Yurka still plays *Gina*, which is as it should be. There is a new *Hedvig*, Miss Linda Watkins, and we doubt that a better one could have been found. The entire cast, as a matter of fact, including Dallas Anderson, Ralph Roeder and John Daly Murphy, help to make this revival a standard at which all the new dramas may aim, if they like, but with scant hope of success.

Another good play which has stood the test of time theatrically better than most of those by the same author is "Macbeth." This will always be good melodrama, and, next to "Hamlet," the best thing of Shakespeare's to see unless you happen to be a member of a high school English class which *has* to see them all. The present production (now on the road) has the added advantage of scenery inspired, if not actually designed, by Gordon Craig (according to a frantic exchange of letters in the daily press, Douglas Ross seems to be responsible for the actual production), and, while there is a plethora of aimless stairways leading nowhere, apparently designed for messengers to fall down, the whole effect is pretty impressive.

Florence Reed makes *Lady Macbeth* just a bit more physically attractive than we generally think of Scotch dames as being, and, in the sleepwalking scene, has gone to Helen Menken's whitewash pot to the extent of resembling an equestrienne in the Barnum and Bailey living-picture groups (without the white horse), but it all goes toward making "Macbeth" a little more stimulating to the eye than heretofore. Lyn Harding's *Macbeth* is sufficiently dumb and heavy to uphold the best Scotch tradition.

After waking up those subscribers who had fallen asleep at "Faust" and forgotten to go home, the Theatre Guild played good and safe and revived Shaw's "Major Barbara" for its second bill. Very few people will fall asleep at "Major Barbara," although there may be stretches when its message sounds a little obvious, owing to its having been taken up by the best people since Shaw wrote it. Between wars the best people are always amenable to Shaw. It is only when a good war is in the offing that it becomes bad form to agree with him. Anybody can enjoy "Major Barbara" now, and not lose caste.

December 14, 1928

THE SEASON'S PEAK

WHAT was supposed to be the peak of the theatrical season came around Christmas time, along with that bracing, tepid Christmas weather. In this season, any slight bulging away from the ground constitutes a peak, and the great December renaissance can hardly be said to have been much more than that.

There was a general air and bustle of great doings along Broadway. Dozens of plays all opened at once (and closed almost immediately); Ethel Barrymore opened a new theatre with a new play; Mr. Belasco printed up a lot of new money and tossed it gravely into the clattering furnace of "The Red Mill" (rechristened "Mima" for short); the Theatre Guild put on a drama containing absolutely no sex appeal (unless matinee audiences can derive excitement from the sight of a British Cabinet meeting at No. 10 Downing Street—and matinee audiences have derived excitement from much less), and everyone was very optimistic and busy.

Out of all this activity, the two productions of the Theatre Guild, "Wings Over Europe" and "Caprice," seem to be the only precipitate worth saving. In itself, "Caprice" is not a play to make any season highly distinguished, but the acting of Lynn Fontanne and Alfred Lunt *is*. Two more delightful performances it would be difficult to get on one stage at the same time. We have gone over all this before, how good we think Miss Fontanne and Mr. Lunt are and, if there had been any opposition, we could now have said "We told you so." But when no one will have an argument with you, all you can do is mutter to yourself "Very good, very good indeed!" We will also mutter a few words of commendation for young Mr. Douglass Montgomery.

The Guild's other offering, "Wings Over Europe," is remarkable in that it has no women in the cast and that no one in his right senses would ever have expected to make a play out of it. So Robert Nichols and Maurice Browne made one and the

Guild put it on and it turns out to be very exciting. It has its weak spots and an occasional one which is a little more than just weak, but when an author writes a play about blowing up the world by a redistribution of atoms he cannot expect to convince his audience any sooner than he could convince the Cabinet of Great Britain. But the whole thing was a very brave venture into theatrical wilds and is easily the most interesting experiment in town. In recommending it, we repeat that no ladies appear on the stage and that at least one lobe of your brain will have to be functioning in order to get the keenest enjoyment from the play. But you won't really be thinking as deeply as you think you are.

Mr. Belasco has taken Molnar's "The Red Mill" and made a gigantic machine of it, into which he has put Lenore Ulric and Sidney Blackmer and called it "Mima." On the whole, we like Mr. Belasco's machinery better than Mr. Molnar's play. Mr. Blackmer, an honest peasant "whom even the silk worms love," is seen in the various stages of moral disintegration in the infernal machine, each stage accompanied by a new gadget from Mr. Belasco's laboratory and a leer of delight from Miss Ulric, who has the satanic appointment as demoralizing agent in charge of Mr. Blackmer.

In the end, however, owing to the young peasant's thinking of his mother or America's debt to France or something, he is saved from complete degradation and the entire machine collapses with considerable dignity. It is all highly impressive and obvious. Mr. Belasco's gadgets, however, and Miss Ulric's various impersonations are always something to watch.

Miss Ethel Barrymore recently complained in a magazine article that the critics gave her credit for only beauty and personality and seldom for skill. She should thank her stars that her beauty and personaltiy were on tap in the first two acts of "The Kingdom of God" and that she could save her skill for the third. The third act is splendid, thanks to this skill, but the first two are pretty terrible.

In the first act, Miss Barrymore is seen as *Sister Gracia* at the age of nineteen, in the second at the age of twenty-nine and in the third at seventy. By the time she is seventy there has been a noticeable improvement in her vocal methods due to advancing age, and that high, breathless monotone which, at nineteen, made it a little difficult to understand just what she was saying, has given way to a rich, full voice which snaps out the words in thrilling fashion.

Miss Barrymore and her much-imitated voice have given rise to a school of acting which might be called the Episcopalian Method. In this, each line is chanted like a response, with no differentiation in tone between lines, and sometimes goes on like that for hours. Now Miss Barrymore does this usually when she thinks the rôle needs it and can shift at will, as she does in the third act of "The Kingdom of God," but it would be too bad if a standard were set whereby young actresses chanted exclusively and one were never again to hear a human voice in natural conversation on the stage. Little as Miss Barrymore esteems her own beauty and personaltiy, they would come in very handy for anyone who wanted to follow in her steps.

January 18, 1929

"DYNAMO"

THOSE few of us who looked with something less than ecstasy on "Strange Interlude" when it appeared on that long afternoon over a year ago, may find a little justification for our scepticism in Mr. O'Neill's latest drama "Dynamo." Nobody who could write "Dynamo" is above being kidded. And "Dynamo" gives the tip-off on "Strange Interlude" and "The Great God Brown". They *were* just as bad as we thought they were. Now we know.

It takes a great deal of concentration on "The Emperor Jones" and "The Hairy Ape" to keep alive the thought that Mr. O'Neill is America's greatest dramatist. Of course, if he isn't, the question arises, "Who is, then?" and we scurry right back to Mr. O'Neill, with apologies. But it does seem too bad that America's greatest dramatist should be a man entirely devoid of humor.

In wishing that Mr. O'Neill had a sense of humor we do not mean that we want him to write humorously or gag up his plays. Nine-tenths of the value of a sense of humor in writing is not in the things it makes one write but in the things it keeps one from writing. It is especially valuable in this respect in serious writing, and no one without a sense of humor should ever write seriously. For without knowing what is funny, one is constantly in danger of being funny without knowing it.

It has long been a characteristic of the O'Neill drama to burlesque itself as it draws toward its close. The first acts, as in "The Great God Brown" and "Desire Under the Elms", fill you with the thrilling hope that here is something great. And then things begin piling up, and Pelion is not only put on Ossa but Mt. Monadnock and a couple of funny-looking hills are added, until the whole thing turns into a comedy. Of course, nobody could tell what the last part of "The Great God Brown" was about, not even Mr. O'Neill, but "Desire Under the Elms" began to get comical when the old gentleman flounced out of the house to go down and sleep with the cows. A sense of humor on Mr. O'Neill's part would have kept him from writing that. (It would also have kept him from writing the last half-dozen "purty, ain't its".)

"Strange Interlude", with its splendid fifth and sixth acts, goes burlesque on itself in that incomparable comedy scene at the boat races when people begin dropping dead, but the first act is no slouch as parody. And the famous "aside" method, which is quite all right if you think you need it to get your point across, in the hands of a man with no humor is always on the verge of being ridiculous and often much nearer than that. With a sense of humor Mr. O'Neill could have made "Strange Interlude" a two-and-a-half hour play and a great one.

It is doubtful if even a sense of humor could have made "Dynamo" a great play but it could have made it less dull and less obvious. Roaming through its maze of random soliloquies, asides, apostrophes and dialogue are some fine things. And the royal blood of the "Count of Monte Cristo", which is always with Mr. O'Neill and which, unlike the daisies, always tells, gives him the power to throw a dramatic spotlight on all his works so that the lurid glow of the theatre lies over even his dullest passages. It is a question if this inheritance from his trouper father is not his most valuable quality as a dramatist. Certainly without it, many of his works would be practically nothing to watch.

"Dynamo", then, has this quality of latent excitement, even if it never comes to much, and Mr. Simonson's Erecto-houses and last-act powerplant help to keep it alive. There is also a character (played by Catherine Calhoun Doucet) which always threatens to come to life—the vapid mother who is struggling with a big idea in a small way, but nothing much is done with her except to leave her petting a dynamo in the inevitable burlesque fashion of most of O'Neill's grand characters.

The rest of the cast performs with the efficiency of all Theatre Guild casts: Glenn Anders, George Gaul, Helen Westley, Dudley Digges and, as an excellent bit of casting, Claudette Colbert. But there are such handicaps imposed on actors by this O'Neill method that it is difficult for even the best to do much more than just recite. It this school of dramatic writing is coming into any vogue at all, we might as well teach our actors to project their voices and let it go at that. There is no sense in trying to act when the only person you have to feed you and talk to is yourself or a piece of scenery.

A while ago to treat a play of Eugene O'Neill's flippantly or, condescendingly, to pick out its good points would have been presumptuous. Another like "Dynamo" and it will be about all we can do. And we are promised two more!

March 8, 1929

THE ELEPHANT WHO
ALMOST FORGOT

T WELVE years ago this month the editor of this department sent in his first contribution to LIFE. It was on the subject of war gardens and was very funny indeed, but it was returned. Twelve years ago next month he sent in his second contribution. It, too, was returned. Both transactions had been on the most formal of bases. The contributions had been accompanied by stamped, self-addressed envelopes and were returned in the same, with identic notes which could have been read aloud in any courtroom with no embarrassment at all to the editors. This sort of thing went on for some time.

At last, convinced that there was a conspiracy against us in the office of LIFE, we (in order not to confuse you longer, we will disclose that the editor of this department mentioned above was none other than we) got pretty darned sore. Tossing and turning one night on what later turned out to be our cot, we worked up an imaginary conversation, in which the editor of LIFE came to us on bended knee and asked us to write something for him. "We have been blind fools, Benchley," he would say. "Won't you let bygones be bygones and do something for us on your own terms?" And our answer, as we figured it out roughly, would be to place our tongue against our under lip and to blow. This would be accompanied by a contemptuous wave of the hand upward and some sort of crushing exit, to be worked up later. "Write for LIFE?" we would say, (this was another version) "Aha-ha-ha! You had your chance. Now lie in it!"

For three years we worked on this conversation until, if we do say so, it was pretty good. Then, just nine years ago this week, the editor of LIFE sent us a note asking us to drop into his office. "Yeah?" we said, "so they are coming to their senses at last! Well, it can do no harm to see what they want." (We had just been fired from the *World*.) So we dropped into the office of LIFE, after rehearsing the gesture of the tongue against the under lip.

It seemed that the Dramatic Editor of LIFE was leaving, and they wanted someone to do the page for a few weeks until they could get a regular man. A very humiliating offer it was, and made to a man who had already been humiliated beyond endurance. So we accepted.

For nine years we have been temporizing with our pride. They didn't want our contributions in 1917. Very well, then, we will write no more for them now! But somehow we never got around to saying it. Things were very pleasant here, and, as the editor who had turned down our stuff left six years ago, there didn't seem to be anyone to whom it could be said. Going to the theatre turned out to be a rather happy chore; nobody told us what we had to write or what we couldn't write; the company's checks were good, and, what with one thing and another, we kept putting off the big scene we had rehearsed, until here it is 1929. But we still cannot forget those returned manuscripts.

Furthermore, we took the job with the understanding that it was to be for only a few weeks. We knew nothing about the theatre at the time and have religiously tried to keep to that standard ever since. We were never cut out to be a dramatic critic. Birds and flowers, with perhaps an occasional horse, are our metier.

Having been so tentatively assigned to the Drama, we have never thought it worthwhile to read any books on the subject or to take seriously the movement as a whole. We know nothing of the history of the theatre and have given practically no thought to its future other than to look into the paper to see what plays were opening Monday night. All of this tells in the long run and we find ourself, at the end of nine years of play-reviewing, even more inexpert than we were at the start. We hope that none of you have ever been taking this page seriously.

So, all in all, it seems better to assert ourself in the matter of those rejected manuscripts and, at the same time, stop trying to do something which was only a stopgap anyway—a nine-year stopgap. And, although our gesture has lost most of its force by having lost all of its rancor and might very easily turn into a short manly sob, there is one thing that we can never forgive the editors of this paper for. When we began on this job we were told, in all sincerity, that our copy *had* to be in by Tuesday night. We now find out, quite by accident, that it really didn't have to be in until Wednesday night. For four hundred and sixty-eight weeks we have been wearing our nerves to shreds in order to have everything in a whole day ahead of what was necessary. And they have been sitting back and laughing at us.

And so, to Mr. McIntyre, who will take up this torch from now on, we offer our best wishes and this advice. "Don't let them kid you, Mr. McIntyre! Wednesday night, at five o'clock, is plenty time enough."

Editorial Note—Now that Mr. Benchley has given up Dramatic Criticism for the Talking Movies we trust, for the sake of synchronization, that his words will be more on time on the screen than they were in this office. But even if he is a little late, we'll probably like it.

March 29, 1929

PART II

THE YEARS AT
THE NEW YORKER
1929–1940

EX POST FACTO

THIS business of opening a play and then closing it just as this department gets the review in type has ceased to be funny.

At first we took the thing in the nature of a good joke on us when a play which opened on Monday closed on the following Saturday, one day after our notice of it had gone to the printer. "Well, we certainly will look silly," we said laughingly, "coming out next Friday with a review of a play which has been closed almost a week!" Things went on for quite a while in this vein. I am a hard man to rile.

But gradually this schedule has become tiresome and threatens to grow irritating shortly. If the managers are trying to wear me down by this policy of closing shows after they have run only a week, they are succeeding. This page has a very definite function, which is to comment on current plays as soon as possible after they open. But if plays stop being current almost immediately after they have opened, we shall have to give this space over to a discussion of more permanent features of our metropolitan life, such as migratory birds or cold spells. We can't go on just registering deaths.

Last week the announcement of the closing of "The Amorous Antic" came just in time for us to change "is" to "was" in the proof. This week, just as we had turned out a rather fine piece of writing on Isadora Duncan (fortunately only in manuscript), the notice appears that "Diana" will close on Saturday (that would be *last* Saturday in your money). Consequently, we are tearing up several sheets of *belles lettres* with considerable regret, not only for the loss to the nation but for the great hole it is going to make in this page. We may have to run a poem to fill.

There is one thing that *can* be said about "Diana," however. Probably eight out of ten people who read the autobiography of Isadora Duncan remarked to themselves: "There is a great play there! Someone ought to write it." And probably five out of each eight started to write it themselves. Out of all these starts, Irving Kaye Davis was the first to finish and reach Broadway with his product. This was too bad, for some of the others must have been better. I was not so upset at the outrage to Isadora Duncan's memory as were many of the reviewers, but I was disappointed that it wasn't a better play. There should be a great play in that vivid, madcap career, and I hope that I do not further affront Isadora Duncan's admirers when I suggest that it be written by Edna Ferber and George Kaufman in much the same spirit as that in which they wrote "The Royal Family." Maybe such a tragi-comedy should be postponed for a few years and even then should eschew such a complete adherence to the facts as Mr. Davis blundered into, but there, I think, lies the real play. The tragic ending would lose nothing by the preceding chaotic comedy, in fact, it would be doubly effective—always provided, of course, that it was well done. There lay the greatest fault of Mr. Davis' play: it was not well done. Let the others who follow take warning.

There is little danger of "Family Affairs" closing before this page reaches your eager hands, because it has Miss Billie Burke in it and she is good for at least a six weeks' buy at any agency, sight unseen. I have never been what you would call a Billie Burke fan, owing to an old, inherited aversion to cuteness, but I must admit that, in her present mood, Miss Burke is at her best. By that I mean that the twittering and trilling and left-shoulder-up-and-right-shoulder-down work have been reduced to a minimum and we find the lady, at a point in her career when one would least expect a reversal of form, being not only modified in her mannerisms but actually charming. And, if she will not mind my saying so, ten years younger-looking than anyone else in the cast. (I mention this only because we have seen so many pictures of Miss Burke with her daughter and of her daughter without Miss Burke that it is an open secret that she is a mother. Otherwise, it would be difficult to believe.)

The play certainly needs Miss Burke if ever a play did. It is a quite unbelievable comedy of what seems to be considered "modern" life, with a set pattern which is made patent at the very beginning and does not disappoint by deviating. Occasionally there are lines which are as good as *all* the lines are intended to be, which makes one wish that not quite such an effort had been made. But when you fix it so that your heroine invites her husband's mistress, her son's lady friend, and her daughter's fiancé all to spend a week in the house together, you have either got to write a perfect comedy or fall pretty flat. And "Family Affairs" is several parasangs from being a perfect comedy. Perhaps its most egregious slip is in offering a young man's card with "Harvard Club" on it as evidence that he is socially beyond reproach.

December 21, 1929

* * *

Those old bibliophiles who save their back copies of THE NEW YORKER may get an ill-natured laugh at this department's expense by turning to page 34 of last week's issue, wherein a prophecy was tossed off. I was complaining of the recent unpleasant habit among managers of closing their shows almost immediately after the final curtain on the opening night, thereby making a monkey out of a page like this which has to go through certain mechanical formalities before it can be printed.

"There is little danger," I said, nodding sagely, "of 'Family Affairs' closing before this page reaches your eager hands, because it has Miss Billie Burke in it and she is good for at least a six weeks' buy at any agency, sight unseen." So the next night after that was written, "Family Affairs," *with* Miss Billie Burke, closed.

O well, the hell with it! Go ahead and close your old shows and see if *I* care! I'll do my duty. I'll get all dressed up and go to the openings. I'll make little notes on my program which I can't read when I get seated at my typewriter, and I'll write out the notices and send them to the printer, just as if there were a real play under consideration. And *then* I shall stop worrying my pretty little head about it. If it closes, all right. If it runs, all right. I don't want to hear about it again, please. And I hope that you, my dear readers, will derive enough inspiration and joy out of merely reading what I have written, regardless of the continued existence of the play, to pay you for coming out in all this rain. Let's just be friends from now on, and not clients and dramatic critics at all. That will be more fun, anyway.

The New Yorker, December 28, 1929

SATIRE TO MUSIC

THERE is a great deal more to "Strike Up the Band" than comical gags and nice music. For one act, at least, it is about as devastating satire as has been allowed on the local boards for a long time I say "allowed" because only a little over eleven years ago it would have landed Messrs. Ryskind, Gershwin, and Selwyn in Leavenworth. Kidding war and war-makers is a sport for which there is an open season and a closed season. The open season is only during those intervals when nobody happens, for the moment, to be wanting to make a war.

The story (originally written by George S. Kaufman and now revised by Morrie Ryskind) of a musical-comedy war with Switzerland over the use of Grade B milk in chocolate involves the presence of several types of super-patriot who were much in evidence in these parts during 1914-18. There were plenty of them in the audience on the opening night and some of the lines spoken for comedy must have sounded vaguely familiar to them. All members of the National Security League should be made to attend "Strike Up the Band"—and not laugh. In fact, those who have a right to laugh are only those who laughed (or cried) at the same things in the days when we were planning a war of our own. Oddly enough, Mr. Ryskind himself is one of the few who come under that heading, having had some trouble at Columbia University for saying much the same things that he is now drawing down royalties for.

Mr. Ira Gershwin's lyrics, too, would have been matter for heavy conferences among the patriotic societies of an earlier day. Any man who would write: "We don't know what we're fighting for, but it really doesn't matter" would bear watching. And incidentally, Mr. Ira Gershwin will bear watching, or listening to, today, for his lyrics are consistently literate, correct, and amusing. I need hardly call attention to the merits of his brother George, who has written for "Strike Up

106

the Band" some of the best things he has done. It is too bad that the show did not come into town when it was first written two years ago, for the score at that time contained "The Man I Love," which later came in all by itself and won more than a passing popularity. But Mr. Gershwin's finale to the first act is fine enough to carry a show without help.

I have left until the last any mention of Bobby Clark because I am told that I made something of a display of myself at the opening by laughing so loudly. If many more newspapers in their play-reviews comment on the noise I make when I laugh, I shall begin to think that there is something in it. I have now in my scrapbook four personal notices on my laugh, not all of them complimentary but all very clearly printed, and I am thinking of having them put on my personal stationery. ("Mr. Benchley's guffaws rising as a sort of overtone over the general merriment."—Arthur Ruhl in the *Herald Tribune*.)

Perhaps after this I need only add that I thought Bobby Clark funny. He has turned from his old-time hand-to-hand encounters with cigar and stick (although he still carries them) and is funny without them. Some time I shall have to sit down and think out the reason why he is so funny. Right now I don't know. But to see him, in a Confederate general's coat and an admiral's hat, executing maneuvers which he counts on to make him physically attractive to a lady, is something very definite in emotional experiences. Mr. McCullough, the only straight-man in the business who dresses up like a comic, is also present, and our old love, Blanche Ring, adds her sure touch to a picture which is already pretty darned good. The second act runs downhill quite a bit, but, having started so high up, it doesn't have time to get very far.

The New Yorker, January 25, 1930

WHAT IS A GOOD SHOW?

I T LOOKS as if we ought to have a man come around from the garage and tighten up our standards of dramatic entertainment. They are getting very loose. By that I do not mean morally loose, but loose in their definitions. We don't seem to be very clear in our minds about what we have a right to expect when we go to the theatre.

For example, we are told that "of course, Shaw's 'The Apple Cart' isn't really a play; it is a dramatized pamphlet," or, "naturally there are long stretches of repetitious talk which do not belong in the theatre, but then that's Shaw." Now if "The Apple Cart" isn't really a play, what is the sense in playing it? If its long speeches do not belong in the theatre, what are they doing in the theatre? Simply because Mr. Shaw happens to be the greatest writer alive, does that give him the right to ask us to accept as dramatic entertainment material which should be read by a reading lamp? There is no law making it compulsory for him to write a play, and if he doesn't want to write a play which will act, he can write a book instead. A play by Shaw can evidently be three days long, have no second act, or be presented by camels carrying letters which spell out the words. One character can do all the talking until he drops dead, or all the characters can talk all at once and all of the time. Every known element which goes into making a play dramatically effective can be disregarded, and yet it is put on as a "play" and we must accept it as such.

Or again, we go to see Mei Lan-fang, the "King of Actors." We are told "of course, you won't understand what he is doing and of course you will be a little bored, but you must make allowances for the entirely different traditions of acting in China and remember that this tradition is two thousand years old."

Why *need* we be bored? Why should we have to make allowances for *anything* when we go for entertainment? Why is it incumbent on the audience which has paid its money for an evening in the theatre to adjust itself to Shaw or to Mei Lan-fang? Other playwrights and other actors have to adjust themselves to their audiences if they want to hold their attention. Granted there is a certain academic interest in what Shaw has to say on Democracy and a certain aesthetic pleasure in watching Mei Lan-fang use his hands for perhaps half an hour. But it isn't a whole evening in the theatre and no amount of "making allowances" can transform it into a whole evening in the theatre. And if it isn't that, why put it in the theatre?

Much of "The Apple Cart" is delightful (but nowhere near so delightful as you are led to believe). A great deal more of it is just plain dull. You would skip great chunks of it if you were reading it. Much of Mei Lan-fang is interesting when you have been told what it means and, if you are in the mood for a dance recital, there are graceful gestures to follow with your rapidly closing eyes. But the fact that Shaw wrote the dull parts of his play does not make them less dull, and dullness has no place in the theatre. And the fact that Mei Lan-fang's falsetto is in accordance with a two-thousand-year-old tradition does not make it less harsh and irritating and tiresome under *any* standards, neither does the knowledge that we have not sufficient culture to understand what he is doing make it any less irksome *not* to understand what he is doing. And irksomeness has no place in the theatre, whether it arises from our provincial ignorance or not. If we are going to let Shaw and Mei Lan-fang get away with boring us, we have got to let other playwrights and actors do it, too. My suggestion would be that *nobody* be allowed to bore us.

Now Marc Connelly has written in "The Green Pastures" a play which is, both in conception and execution, so much finer than "The Apple Cart" as a play that there is no basis for comparison. And he has put into it more beauty than twenty Mei Lan-fangs could get out of twenty Chinese plays even if they were *four* thousand years old instead of two. And yet we hold Mr. Connelly pretty strictly to account, and if there are signs of the almost incredibly high standard of his first act sagging a bit in his second, he must answer to us for it. Mr. Shaw can write any old kind of tract and call it a "play," but Mr. Connelly must write a perfect play or we will have none of it. Well, Mr. Connelly has done just about that.

I do not remember ever crying before over the thing that made me cry almost continuously at "The Green Pastures." I cried because here was something so good. As the story of the Creation and Man's Fall and the Flood, told in terms of an ignorant Negro's imagination, unfolded itself in a series of eighteen scenes, beginning with a "fish fry" in Heaven (at which one of the smallest colored angels on record gets a fish

109

bone caught in its throat) and ending with another "fish fry" at which God (in the almost unbearably lovable person of a colored preacher) accepts the destiny which comes even to divine rulers, one realized that here was something not only new for the theatre but something good for the theatre. It is a fine, fine thing that Mr. Connelly has written.

The all-Negro cast which he has directed could not possibly be better. With material such as this to work with, their natural feeling for the theatre makes itself doubly manifest. As there are almost a hundred of them, including several extremely small angels and children of Israel, one can hardly mention all who deserve mention, but Richard B. Harrison, with a voice like Walter Huston's and a presence which radiates beneficence and proud humility, makes the rôle of the Lord one which not only is not sacrilegious but is excellent propaganda for the Christian Church. If the Lord is really anything like Mr. Harrison, maybe I have been wrong all these years.

There must be a word for the settings which Robert Edmond Jones has done. They, too, are in the spirit of the play, resembling the conventional southern Negro's idea of a stage Heaven in terms of old New Orleans Opera House flats and flies, and yet modern in their effect—a pretty difficult job of designing, you will admit.

You have never seen anything like "The Green Pastures" in the theatre before, and you are not likely to see anything like it again, for it could not be imitated. And if you don't see if now, you don't deserve to.

The New Yorker, March 8, 1930

WITH LOVE FROM THE GREEK

THE most important New York theatrical event of the spring took place in Philadelphia. In fact, it is still taking place there, and I would recommend a trip to what may be, for the nonce, called the City of Bodily Love for all those who have even a half-hearted interest in modern staging and classical comedy. It may not come into New York, unless some far-seeing manager has nerve enough to bring it, and you will never forgive yourself for having missed it.

An organization called the Philadelphia Theatre Association were the ones to put New York to shame. They got Gilbert Seldes to make an English version of the "Lysistrata" of Aristophanes and gave Norman-Bel Geddes the necessary thousands of dollars to make a superlative production of it. They also took, right out from under our local noses, such experts as Fay Bainter, Ernest Truex, Miriam Hopkins, Sydney Greenstreet, Hortense Alden, and Eric Dressler, to say nothing of a great many young men and women to dance under the direction of Doris Humphrey and Charles Weidman, and put them all together in the Walnut Street Theatre for a festival of beauty and bawdiness such as has, I venture to say, never been seen on an American stage before.

A subsidiary group of the Moscow Art Theatre did "Lysistrata" several years ago in New York, but they did it in Russian, which eliminated the fun, and they did not utilize Mr. Geddes' talents, which eliminated the beauty. You would not recognize it as the same show. As it stands, it is something quite new and thrilling for our theatre.

There is no use in trying to make allowances for "Lysistrata" to those who are easily shocked, or even to those who are shocked at all. It is frankly and openly a comedy of sex, and, it seems to me, by its very frankness and openness, quite clean. The story of the Athenian and Spartan women who end a war by denying themselves to their husbands and lovers until peace is assured could not be told

111

by innuendoes and sly leering. Aristophanes came right out and said it in Greek, and Mr. Seldes, always within certain broad limits of good taste, has come right out and said it in English, and the result is a strange clearing of the atmosphere and an almost prophylactic sanity. It may be that Philadelphia audiences are more civilized than New York's, but I did not hear a titter or see a nudge during the entire performance, only loud, clear, and entirely healthy laughter. Perhaps the subject of sex is not quite so nasty as we have been led to believe—who knows?

Of course, the production itself has a great deal to do with it. Mr. Geddes has never done a more beautiful or exciting piece of staging. There are at least a dozen moments during the evening which take your breath away or bring tears to your eyes according to your personal reaction to beauty. Merely the picture of the two Athenian women coming up over the brow of the hill bearing the enormous votive bowl for their oath of renunciation is something to take back to New York with you to remember. And the grand bacchanalia with which the plays ends is almost too much for one pair of eyes to bear. I do hope that I am not being too aesthetic about this thing.

The actors also seem to have been caught up by the spirit of Mr. Geddes' lavishness and give the performances of their lives. Mr. Truex is a marvel of thwarted virility and when, almost completely hidden by his shield and helmet (the latter on hindside-before) he threatens to spite the women of Athens by "ploughing through every brothel in town," there is nothing left to do but unfurl banners and march up and down the aisles. Miss Bainter, although not quite the Athenian type, makes up for it by her clear understanding of the subtlety of the comedy, and the Misses Hopkins and Alden, simply by looking as they do, make the plight of the men of Athens seem almost too pitiful to be borne. No war could be worth that price.

If New York doesn't get this production of "Lysistrata" it is crazy. Any city which can stand "Little Orchid Annie" without impairment to its morals has no right to raise an eyebrow at Aristophanes. And if Philadelphia is to be the only city which has the perception and courage to take Mr. Seldes and Mr. Geddes and give them encouragement, then this department will make that city its headquarters from now on. (*Flood of letters saying "O.K."*)

The New Yorker, May 10, 1930

PRELIMINARY LECTURE

I N TAKING up the work for the new year, I would like to remind the class that this is not going to be what you boys call a "snap course." We have a great deal of ground to cover, some of it on our hands and knees, and we can have no laggards, no dull-wits. You will all have to pay strict attention and make just the neatest, neatest notes, while I, in my turn, will do my very best to keep awake. And, always remember, there is, as yet, no state law compelling you to take this course if you don't like it.

In this connection, it has been the custom hitherto in this course to interrupt Teacher when there were any questions to be asked or complaints to be registered. From now on Teacher does not want to be interrupted. Teacher gets awfully tired standing on his feet all day over a hot desk, and you may be quite sure that he is doing the very best that he can. He does not pretend to know any more about the course than you do. He is just here to make it easier for you to stay away from the theatre, and to furnish you with names and dates, many of them incorrect. But when he makes a mistake, he knows it a long, long time before you catch it, and, you may rest assured, worries himself into a neurasthenia over it. And, insofar as it is possible, he will correct it.

And if, by any chance, you are tempted to question him concerning his venality or log-rolling, it will be worth your while to count to one hundred first, for it is going to make him increasingly cross and irritable. If he had been venal during the past ten years he wouldn't be working now, and if he had rolled logs, he wouldn't be practically friendless as he now is. So, when anything pops into your mind which you might possibly use to bother Teacher with, remember: "Don't Write—Don't Telegraph!"

And now we will take a little recess before beginning the hard grind of the term, and all cluster together in the front of the room where Teacher will dictate to you

113

the words to the French version of the "Maine Stein Song" which he heard that loyal Maine alumna Mistinguett sing only a few short weeks ago in Paris. You must remember that the literal translation is printed on the music just below the original words of Mr. Lincoln Colcord, which begin: "Fill the steins to dear old Maine." The title on the cover is "La Petite Femme de Paris. Stein Song. (University of Maine)" and we will now fill the tankards and raise them on high in the following tribute to the grand old university at Orono:

> C'est la p'tit' femme de Paris
> Quie gracieuse et coquett—e
> Met d'l'amour dans tous les esprits
> Et fait tourner toutes les têt—es.
> Oui, et quand un coeur est pris,
> Par la p'tit' femme qui pass—e
> De Montmartre à Montparnass—e
> C'est un' petit' femm' de Paris.

[Now comes the part beginning "To the trees, to the sky," etc., and try and sing it, you think you know so much French.]

> Des minois ravissants, d'jolis teints,
>   éclatants, des sourires charmants,
> Des cheveux merveilleux, tous les yeux
>   noirs ou bleus ont l'air malicieux.
> Tous c'qu'on voit c'est joli, c'est
>   mignon, c'est gentil, les yeux sont
>   ravis.
> Ce qu'elle a de meilleur, mais que l'on
>   ne voit pas, c'est son coeur!
> Oui! ["Boom" in English.]
> [Repeat chorus, with bared heads.]

I want every one in the class to have this learned before the next meeting of the course, for we are going to open the lecture with it and may do nothing else during the entire hour but sing it. And you don't want to be the only one who doesn't know it, do you?

The New Yorker, August 30, 1930

114

HURRAH FOR US!

THERE is no denying it: when you Americans put your minds to a thing, you do it up brown. The things that you *do* may not be so hot, but you certainly do them right, and I think you are a wonderful, wonderful little people. *There*, now I've said it!

In what other country of the world could you find, for example, an old Punch and Judy show like "Princess Charming" transformed into such a magnificent and glowing affair that, for at least one act, you are hypnotized into thinking it a great show? Where else could a regulation musical-comedy framework like "Girl Crazy" receive such expert treatment and loving care that it rises off the ground under its own power and soars around shooting off rockets and ringing bells? And above all, where would you find a revue like "Three's a Crowd"?

England (meaning Noel Coward) might produce a revue with as clever skits and pretty songs as the last-mentioned but it is doubtful if any English producer would unbelt to the extent that Mr. Max Gordon has in the matter of costumes, scenery, and all the other little Cartier knicknacks which Hassard Short, because he likes nice things, is accustomed to work with. A French revue might possibly be as well dressed, but its sketches and songs would be, unless a new race of men has sprung up in France since July, god-awful. A German revue might have the same easy-going rompery and even a better score, but it wouldn't be worth opening your eyes to look at. The only Russian review I know anything about is the "Chauve Souris," and I spent four years in Leavenworth Prison for walking out on that.

So, you see, we are a pretty satisfactory old nation after all—at any rate, when it comes to producing revues like "Three's a Crowd." Here we have the same triumvirate (if Miss Libby Holman doesn't mind being called a *vir* for a minute, just to make it easier for me) which made the first "Little Show" the show it was:

Clifton Webb, Fred Allen, and Miss Holman. There is also Mr. Howard Dietz, who helped on that first job and has taken over this one completely to write the lyrics, harvest the sketches, and, in general, to contribute lavishly from one of the few civilized senses of humor on Broadway today.

The three stars had a pretty tough spot to come into after the glowing notices they received at the opening of the "Second Little Show," in which they were not. Fortunately, they were more than equal to the crisis. Mr. Allen now takes his place as the master monologist of the pre-Repeal era, and from the moment when he enters, explaining his tardiness by saying that he has been down to the station seeing two magistrates off, until he closes the show with a brotherly imitation of Mr. Webb, there is practically no moment when he is not at top form (which is top form for the course). And at such moments as he is telephoning, in Lawrence Schwab's sketch (this is getting complicated—Lawrence Schwab is a producer of other shows), and sticking handfuls of little burrs in the hide of a well-known pole-flier, he is superb.

I must here put in a word for what bids fair to become one of my favorite characters in the American drama, a small member of Rear Admiral Allen's brave band who never speaks a word, owing doubtless to the fact that he has no face. He is more of a Santa Claus than anything else, and is terrifically sensitive to criticism. The name of this character in the play is simply "Malcolm Weir" and I am madly in love with him.

Miss Holman's voice is even more far-reaching in its effect than last year and her elevation to stardom has given her a new quietness and poise which do nothing to detract. I do not think that her big number, "Body and Soul," is a very good song (it was imported from England quite a long time ago and has had its edge worn off by several hundred saxophones); in fact, none of her numbers is as good as "Moanin' Low" or "Can't We Be Friends?," but Miss Holman herself makes up for whatever unfavorable balance there may be. And Mr. Webb—Mr. Webb hasn't changed a bit, for there was no need for Mr. Webb to change. His comedy, especially in "Je T' Aime" (kindness of Mr. Dietz and Arthur Schwartz), and his dancing at any number of given points make him the ideal keystone for the trio, provided trios have keystones.

And how smart the management of "Three's a Crowd" was to deny the handclappers their quota of encores. The opening-night performance would still be going on if the audience had had its clamorous way.

"Girl Crazy," as one tells about it, sounds like any other musical comedy that one tells about. "Well, it's on this dude ranch in Arizona, and this fellow is in love with this girl—" and there you are. It really has to be seen to get the quality which makes it such a good show, for its chief assets are pace and finesse and the elimination of most of those tiresome interludes which are in the schedule of so many operettas of its class. George Gershwin has written some good numbers, and Ira, his brother, has fitted some excellent words to them, and a young lady named Ethel Merman does wonders with three of them, sustaining one splendid note in "I Got Rhythm" over a period of time usually allotted to the trumpets in orchestration. Ginger Rogers and Allen Kearns also do nicely with a number which Ira Gershwin made his first mistake in calling "Embraceable You" and then made up for by writing the lyric for it.

Willie Howard, without Brother Eugene, takes care of all the comedy there is and adds quite a lot of his own, which is all right with me. He can go on and on as far as he likes, especially if he dresses up as a Jewish Indian to do it. And, as for a strange quartette of gentlemen who roam on and off singing "I'm bidin' my time—that's the kind of guy I'm," I want a whole show of them some day.

The New Yorker, October 25, 1930

INTERMISSION

ONE SUNDAY night, a few months ago, while idly thumbing the dials of my radio set, I was surprised and pleased to hear the words "dramatic critics" issuing forth from the air, spoken in tones which were evidently those of a young lady of intelligence and charm. It was the first time that I had ever heard any words over the radio which were even remotely connected with my own existence, and I was, for all practical purposes, agog. On listening further, I discovered that the young lady unfortunately was very cross at dramatic critics, but, as she seemed to have several constructive suggestions to make for the improvement of the present low state of play-reviewing, I continued to listen, although blushing furiously.

There was one suggestion made by the young lady which impressed me as being particularly sound. It was that dramatic reviews be limited to about fifty words and that they deal with only three items: (1) who was in the play, (2) what it was about, and (3) how it was received. Beyond this the reviewer had no right, even granting him the equipment, to go. To me it sounded like an excellent idea, I being more the lethargic type and not inclined to write any more than is absolutely necessary.

At the conclusion of the philippic, it was announced that we had been listening to Miss Helen Hayes, then playing in "Mr. Gilhooley." As Miss Hayes has now opened in another play, I am fortunately able to combine a compliance with her whim with a short seasonable holiday from writing. It is going to be a little difficult to get all that Miss Hayes allows into fifty words, but I will do my best:

"Petticoat Influence," under the direction of Gilbert Miller, opened at the Empire Theatre on December 15. The story, written by Neil Grant, deals with a young English matron who helps her husband to get his appointment as governor of an island in the Pacific by threatening nicely to blackmail the wife of a Cabinet minister and by exerting her charms on the Cabinet minister himself to such an extent that he takes the appointment away from his wife's uncle, to whom he had already given it, and presents it to the young husband.

In addition to Miss Hayes, the cast includes Henry Stephenson, Reginald Owen, John Williams, Valerie Taylor, and Eric Cowley.

The play was pleasantly received.

(I am sorry to have used more than twice the number of words allotted by Miss Hayes, but I don't see how it could have been avoided.)

Miss Hayes *would* pick a week for her opening in which there was absolutely nothing else to write about, thereby putting me in quite a tough spot. "Petticoat Influence" was the sole première of last week. However, we must comply with the lady's wishes at all costs, even if the rest of this page has to be given over to a discussion of the several moot questions which have been upsetting the theatrical world for the past six weeks. I have done my best to keep away from these subjects, even going so far as to refrain scrupulously from reading a word about them in the newspapers, but I see no other way now but to issue a pronunciamento. The fact that I know nothing about them need not necessarily disqualify me.

In the matter of the sale of theatre tickets I have held myself aloof from absorbing information not so much out of perversity as an inability to keep up with the new schemes as they are announced. As I understand it now, the public can buy good seats for any show in town at a reasonable price by one of the following methods:

(1) Call the Chief Operator of the New York Telephone Company and say, speaking directly into the mouthpiece: "I want two seats for (name of play)." Then shut your eyes and, in a flash, you will find yourself in at least one of the seats.

(2) Cable to the Paris office of the Postal Telegraph Company, using the following code message: "Tooseatsfor (name of play)." Paris will then get in touch with the League offices in Geneva, where your application will be submitted at the next meeting of the Sub-Committee on Orchestra Seats.

(3) Use one of the Western Union holiday forms for Christmas applications, such as: "It is my sincere wish that you and your box office be happy enough to set aside two in the fifth row during this glad Yuletide," or "The season's greetings to you and yours and how about a couple on the aisle for Wednesday night." Send this to the management of the play you wish to see and wait for a reply.

(4) Walk up and down Broadway until you find a ticket agency which has a gold and blue shield pasted on the window. This is a Guelph agency and does not handle

tickets for the show you want to see. The Ghibelline agencies are marked with red and silver shields and they don't handle your tickets either. So stop walking up and down Broadway.

(5) Go to the box office and give the man behind the glass a good laugh.

(6) Call up the same old agency you have always called up, get the two seats you have always got, and pay the same extra smackers you have always paid.

This information is given to readers of this department without any assurance that they will be able to get tickets even then. Next week we will take up the subject of Stage Censorship, about which we know nothing also.

The New Yorker, December 27, 1930

MORE LIKE IT

U P AROUND Massachusetts way there weren't many cowboys or what are hailed as "American folk types, sprung from the soil," so I am not acquainted first-hand with American folk songs or figures of speech. The only American types in New England had been there for two hundred years and had stopped talking. Naturally they could not be considered so indigenous to America as the cowboys in the Indian Territory in 1900. To be *bona-fide* "folk," you have to sing and talk continuously.

I have never heard a cowboy ballad yet that wasn't at least five verses too long, nor have I heard an "American folk speech" on the stage that wasn't at least five words too long. This latter may be the fault of the authors who transcribe the talk of those wide-open spaces which are the only true America (having been taken from Mexico within the last hundred years), but I am inclined to believe, judging from the cowboy ballads, each one of which lasts from 10 P.M. until shortly after midnight, that these rich, loamy types were pretty verbose. I have often wondered, in fact, how they ever got any time to punch cows, what with their singing and piling words one on another.

In "Green Grow the Lilacs" we have a stageful of these loquacious cowboys who, when they are not cutting figures of speech, are singing "Good Bye, Old Paint" or "Home on the Range." It makes up into a rather pleasant entertainment, interspersed with an olio of folk dancing (they were great ones for dancing 'round and 'round) and recitations. After a while it gets just a little tiresome, just as the fun following a "church sociable" in Massachusetts used to get tiresome, and for exactly the same reasons. But one is "folk dancing" and the other is just a lot of people you know acting silly.

It must be admitted, however, that in "Green Grow the Lilacs," Lynn Riggs has come at least ten miles nearer to writing a play than he did in "Roadside." He has chopped off sixteen or eighteen words from each sentence, and very few of them scan. The comedy also has been lifted out of the primary grades and is now in the burlesque-show class, with a fat girl and a Jewish comic made up like Joe Welch. And, in the matter of melodrama, he has caught up with the best of them, so much so that we sit in crouching apprehension waiting a whole scene for two shots to be fired. Some of his melodramatic suspense doesn't quite come off, as in the somewhat duddy attempt at burning two people alive, but the suspense has been there, at any rate, which is more than can be said for the plots of the ballads.

Mr. Riggs is a poet (I am taking the word of other commentators on this point, although I have a sneaking feeling that he has simply a poetic turn of mind. "If I was to drink the gall of a turkey gobbler's liver" is a line picked at random which shows a desire to get away from prose and yet which is not quite poetry—I *think*) but he is not half so much of a poet as he was in "Roadside," which is why "Green Grow the Lilacs" is a far better play.

The Theatre Guild may be responsible for some of this progress in dramatic feeling by Mr. Riggs. It has given his new play an excellent production. It is more in the nature of a musical show, especially in the way the crowds dissolve instantaneously from swirling, shouting mobs of merrymakers into a suddenly silent offstage menace. There is also a Sammy Lee chorus routine which lends a professional note to the indigenous American proceedings. But with Helen Westley doing the best job of her protean career, and June Walker, in spite of the handicap of some impossible cantos to recite, making the young girl a believable and appealing maiden of the plains, with Franchot Tone to make lyric love to her between song cues, Mr. Riggs has fared very well indeed at the hands of the Guild. It does seem a little strange, however, that, in a show which derives most of its lifeblood from singing, Richard Hale should be the only one who doesn't sing.

The most readable review that could be written of Noel Coward's "Private Lives" would be one composed entirely of quotations from the play. And yet, without Mr. Coward or Miss Gertrude Lawrence to read them, they would lose much of their value. The combination of Mr. Coward's lines and his own and Miss Lawrence's delivery makes as hilarious an evening as you can spend in New York today.

The plot is nothing, so we need bother with it no more than Mr. Coward did. A husband and wife, divorced, meet each other on their second honeymoons and— you know how it goes. But what you don't know is how Mr. Coward, by a turn of the head or an inflection of the voice, can make you think you have never heard anything quite so funny in your life. And what you certainly don't know is that Gertrude Lawrence has definitely abandoned her musical-comedy technique and turned into one of the most subtle and effective comédiennes we have. (I say "we," for, since Mr. Harkness has given so much money to England, the least they can do is share Miss Lawrence with us.) And Jill Esmond and Laurence Olivier seem to be just right to trim ship with Miss Lawrence and Mr. Coward, although it is a rather thankless task. To add to all this, the little song which Mr. Coward has written to fill in between laughs is much nicer than anything in our current musical scores.

That's about all there is to say about "Private Lives," I'm afraid.

The New Yorker, February 7, 1931

(*Editor's note*: Rodgers and Hammerstein's "Oklahoma!", which opened on Broadway in 1943, was based on Lynn Riggs' "Green Grow the Lilacs.")

"THE BAND WAGON"

T HE SUMMER theatrical season, up until now on a par with the summer elk season for excitement, has suddenly burst forth into something distinctly resembling splendor, as nearly as we can remember splendor in the summer theatre. It may all be due to seeing a lot of bright lights again, but I have a feeling that things are going to be a lot better from now on, thanks to Max Gordon and Dwight Wiman and their two shows At any rate, things are going to *seem* better.

Of course, the chief impression of splendor comes from Mr. Gordon's "The Band Wagon." Here is a production! I do not know whether it cost a lot of money or not, but it could have cost a million dollars and not have been any better. And furthermore, even on the opening night everything worked. We used to have a lot of fun with Hassard Short because of his elevators and teetering tableaux, but that was evidently just a phase, like whistling through the teeth or playing the mandolin. Mr. Short, backed up by Albert Johnson's backdrops and Howard Dietz' imagination, has emerged from under the old-time piles of gold brocade, bearing with him the practically perfect production.

Lest you get the impression that "The Band Wagon" is nothing but a trip through the Petit Trianon, let us hasten to add that it enlists the services of any number of sterling performers. I have had occasion before, or perhaps I have gone out of my way to take occasion, to toss the old forage cap high in the air over the dancing of Mr. Fred Astaire. So far as I am concerned it is still up in the air, relieving me of the necessity of tossing it again at this point. But it is as comic that Mr. Astaire blossoms forth in "The Band Wagon," and a comic worthy to play alongside his comical little sister Adele, which is no faint praise, as she is at her best here. As the backward Southern boy commenting without emotion on the mighty fine "baudy o' wauter" or the German lieutenant singing "I Love Louisa" (and I defy anybody to witness that gay merry-go-round finale to the first act and still worry about Russian wheat-dumping), Mr. Astaire becomes one of the most valuable pieces of theatrical property in the business. He also plays the accordion.

Another surprise for those of us who have followed Frank Morgan from his early sneering villainies through his high comedy in "The Firebrand" into the paths of his Topaze is the tonal quality of the singing voice in such rich, fruity numbers as "Nanette" (in full quartet) or his lament with Miss Astaire on being miserable together (hey-hey). Is there no limit to this man's powers?

Helen Broderick has already gone down on the records as being one of my weaknesses. She does not always have the best material in a show, but she always has the best way of handling it. Which is probably the reason she is given most of the suggestive lines to read. You may take them or leave them; as for Miss Broderick, she leaves them. And she can make a tall man look smaller than any woman in the world.

The weak part of "The Band Wagon," if any show so obviously in the prime of health can be said to have weak parts, is the sketches. In the opening of the show (which you must under no circumstances miss) there is a burlesque of the ordinary revue so devastating as to make the ordinary revue producer shoot himself if he had any sense. In it a great deal of justifiable kidding is levelled at the conventional blackout. But the blackout, banal as it has become, has its advantages. It at least brings the sketch to a close, a trick which seems to have eluded Mr. Kaufman and Mr. Dietz (of all people!). The sketches themselves have as funny lines in them as have ever been heard in revue sketches, but, like the tell-tale wineglass in the murder-mystery sketch, they have false bottoms. And, while we are on this subject, if I did not know both authors personally, I would have suspected that one or both had some very definite scatological complex, so concerned are they, in a boyish fashion, with matters which hitherto have concerned the J. L. Mott Company alone. They are not particularly offensive, unless you happen to feel them so, but it is certain that the two best satirists that our theatre has today must have more mature ideas to kid about. However, Messrs. Kaufman and Dietz (and, according to the program, the entire production was under Mr. Dietz' supervision, which should elect him President easily) have done enough to mark them as wondermen in the theatre.

We have space enough only to mention the other features of "The Band Wagon," such as Tilly Losch's lovely dancing (the opera-house ballet with Mr. Astaire being sensational, thanks also to Mr. Johnson's setting), the very nice music by Arthur Schwartz, who is at his best in the simple peasant tunes such as "Hoops" and "I Love Louisa:" the protean versatility of Philip Loeb, and the hundred and one other items which go to make "The Band Wagon" the year's top.

The New Yorker, June 13, 1931

HOW I SPENT MY VACATION

MR. ST. JOHN ERVINE, late guest critic on the even later New York *World*, has solved the problem of what to write about during the dull theatrical season. For the past few weeks he has been giving over his dramatic column in the London *Observer* to "A Visit to Scandinavia," or what, in the old grammar-school days, we would have called "My Happiest Vacation Trip." It is fascinating.

There is no item in Mr. Ervine's itinerary too mild for him to record for his eager readers in the *Observer*. Once in a while he goes to a theatre and now and again mentions Ibsen and Björnson, both local boys, just to give his correspondence a racy theatrical flavor. ("You do not know, so I will now tell you," he writes, "that Ibsen and Björnson, who had been college chums, sometimes were furious friends and sometimes were furious enemies." As a matter of fact, Mr. Ervine, I *did* know, so don't get so cocky.) But for the most part "A Visit to Scandinavia" is a little travel essay, with topographical notes and minor reactions to weather and public monuments. (Needless to say, letters have already begun coming in to the *Observer* from irate Norwegians whom Mr. Ervine has offended.)

To quote again from the column, which goes under the name of "At the Play":

"It is, I understand, a great sin, according to the sophisticated, to show any signs of interest in a foreign city, but what do I care what sophisticated persons think or say? (Good for *you*, Mr. Ervine; don't let them bully you!) If I want to gape, I shall gape. . . .I resolved to be what Americans call a rubber-neck. . . .When a thing interests me, I shall look at it, though all the hosts of highbrows politely sneer. I have met persons of this sort whose knowledge of the cities they have seen is limited to the night clubs in which they gyrated and sipped cocktails. I *should* worry if that sort of fool called me a rubber-neck!"

It is doubtful if any Americans who used the word "rubber-neck" would still be young enough to be gyrating in a night club, although they may have taught Mr. Ervine to say "I should worry" with the accent on "should." But that is neither here nor in Oslo. The point is that when a dramatic critic of Mr. Ervine's standing can fill his column "At the Play" with travel notes of almost classic unimportance, I guess that I don't have to worry about how to fill a column headed "The Theatre" when I have just come back from an exciting trip to New Bedford, Massachusetts, by boat.

We left New York from the foot of one of those streets, Chambers, Fulton, Cortlandt, I never can remember which, although I suppose that the smart Algonquin crowd knows every one by heart and will sneer at me behind my back for my honesty in admitting my ignorance. It was a warm afternoon in June, almost *too* warm for comfort, but I had taken the precaution to remove my waistcoat before leaving my hotel and, although I may not have presented as smart an appearance as some of the super-sophisticated log-rollers of my acquaintance, I was comfortable, and that was the main thing. Waistcoats and cheap witticisms are not the only things in life.

The steamer which bore us was called the Providence, a fact which struck me odd at the time considering that we were not going to Providence at all but to New Bedford. I immediately complained to the captain, who was rather surly about the thing (doubtless belonging to one of the New York cliques who have it "in" for me), but he did finally condescend to inform me that the Providence used to run to Providence, Rhode Island, and that the New Bedford boat was the Chester W. Chapin, but that the two had been what the Americans call "swapped" and that the Chester W. Chapin now runs to Providence and the Providence to Chester W. Chapin. I thanked him curtly, giving him just as good as he sent, and went below.

Once we had set sail, a cool breeze came up, which made it necessary for me to take my waistcoat out of my bag and put it on, but I was up to the emergency and soon was quite warm enough. In fact, I was a little *too* warm, so I went below again and took the waistcoat off, effecting a rather ingenious compromise by buttoning my jacket very tightly up over my chest. By this time, we were well around the foot of Manhattan Island, where I could get a good view of the tall buildings on one side (the left) and of Governor's Island on the other (the right). This pleased me immensely.

But we were soon to make another turn and proceed up the East, or Hudson, River (which is also called the "North River," after the confusing fashion of Americans,

127

who seem so intent on making money and "bunny-hugging" and "turkey-trotting" that they have no time left for such old-fashioned things as points of the compass. Thank God I am not so steeped in mental filth that I cannot tell north from south!). Under the Brooklyn Bridge we sailed and I noted that it was a bridge of the suspension type, 113 feet above the water and 6,855 feet long. I am interested in everything.

As I sat on the deck and watched the other bridges drift by over my head (the Manhattan, the Williamsburg, the Queensboro, and the Hell Gate) I thought of the two plays which had opened in New York the week before I left ("The Wooden Soldier" and "Paid Companions"), neither of which was worth thinking any more about. So I stopped thinking of them and devoted my attention to the many interesting sights which were presented along the shores of the river. I will describe more of these, together with my personal reactions to them, in my next week's article, and you may be sure that I shall not mince matters or kow-tow to the Smart Alecs. Any of my readers who do not want to wait until next week before hearing more about my trip may obtain galley proofs of my article in advance by sending to the Ho Hum Department of this paper.

The New Yorker, July 4, 1931

"MOURNING BECOMES ELECTRA"

I N THE midst of the acclaim with which Eugene O'Neill is being so justly hailed for his latest and most gigantic *tour de force*, "Mourning Becomes Electra," and in the confusion of cross-references to the Greek dramatists from whom he derived his grim and overpowering story, are we not forgetting one very important source of his inspiration, without which he might perhaps have been just a builder of word-mountains? Was there not standing in the wings of the Guild Theatre, on that momentous opening night, the ghost of an old actor in white wig, with drawn sword, who looked on proudly as the titanic drama unfolded itself, scene by scene, and who murmured, with perhaps just the suggestion of a chuckle: "That's good, son! Give 'em the old Theatre!"? The actor I refer to needs no introduction to the older boys and girls here tonight—Mr. James O'Neill, "The Count of Monte Cristo" and the father of our present hero.

Let us stop all this scowling talk about "the inevitability of the Greek tragedy" and "O'Neill's masterly grasp of the eternal verities" and let us admit that the reason why we sat for six hours straining to hear each line through the ten-watt acoustics of the Guild Theatre was because "Mourning Becomes Electra" is filled with good, old-fashioned, spine-curling melodrama. It is his precious inheritance from his trouper-father, his father who counted "One," "Two," "Three" as he destroyed his respective victims, one at the curtain to each act; it is his supreme sense of the Theatre in its most elementary appeal, which allows Eugene O'Neill to stand us on our heads (perhaps our heads would have been more comfortable) and keep us there from five in the afternoon until almost midnight. In this tremendous play he gives us not one thing that is new, and he gives us nothing to think about (unless we are just beginning to think), but he does thrill the bejeezus out of us, just as his father used to, and that is what we go to the theatre for.

Just run over in your mind the big scenes in "Mourning Becomes Electra." A daughter upbraiding her mother for adultery, the mother plotting with her lover the murder of her husband, the poisoning of the husband and the discovery of the tablets in the fainting mother's hand, the placing of the tablets on the breast of the corpse to frighten the mother into a confession (and what a scene *that* was!), the brother and sister peering down the hatch of a sailing ship to spy on the mother and later to murder her lover, and the tense moments of waiting for the offstage shots which would tell of the successive suicides of the mother and the brother. Greek tragedy, my eye! The idea may have been the Greeks', but the hand is the hand of Monte Cristo. If the Greek idea of revenge, murder, incest, and suicide is so thrilling, why isn't Margaret Anglin busier than she is? "Mourning Becomes Electra" is just the old Greek story put into not particularly convincing New England talk, but it is a hundred times better show than "Electra" because O'Neill has a God-given inheritance of melodramatic sense. So let's top kidding ourselves about the Verities and the Unities and take a grand, stupendous thriller when we find it and let it go at that.

In the face of such an overwhelming victory over Time, Space, and the Daily Press as that which Mr. O'Neill has won, it is perhaps puny in a single commentator to admit such a personal reaction as fatigue during the last of the three sections of the drama (for they are *not* three plays, as advertised, but one play in fourteen successive acts). But, willing as the spirit may be to take punishment, the human frame is not equipped for such a session as that which is imposed upon it in the Guild Theatre (at any rate, mine isn't, and I have a pretty good equipment), and, starting with a pretty bad scene (go ahead, strike me dead, Jove!) of comic relief at the beginning of the section called "The Haunted," I began to be cushion-conscious. This uneasiness was heightened as I saw approaching that margin of Diminishing Returns in Tragedy which I alone seem to be conscious of in O'Neill's dramas, when one more fell swoop of Fate, one more killing, one more father in love with one more daughter, or one more sister in love with one more brother, and the whole thing becomes just a bit ridiculous. It was when I saw those magnificent scenes of the middle section becoming confused with a grand finale of bad comedy, incest, and extra suicide that Miss Brady's agonized cry, "I couldn't bear another death!," struck home, and I began to realize that, for me personally, "Mourning Becomes Electra" was getting to be just about one hour too long. I know that this is a purely individual and unworthy reaction, quite out of place in what should be a serious review of a great masterpiece, but, as this page is nothing if not personal, I am setting it down. And the final scene of all, in which Electra, or Lavinia, closes herself up in the great New England Greek temple for the rest of her unhappy life, content that mourning is her *métier*, made up for everything.

And now we come to Miss Brady and to Alla Nazimova and to all the rest of the splendid cast which the Theatre Guild has assembled to do homage to Mr. O'Neill's *magnum opus*. Without them, and without Robert Edmond Jones' superb settings, I am not so sure just how effective this drama would be. I can imagine its being pretty bad, as a matter of fact, if only moderately well done. We thrill to the scenes between the mother and daughter on the steps of the cold New England mansion, but how much credit do we give to Mr. Jones and to Mr. Moeller, who gave us this picture of two women in black on the white steps of a Greek temple? (It may have been so nominated in the script, but without Mr. Jones to give it being, it might have remained just a stage-directon.) Alice Brady has at last come into her own, in voice and bearing the perfect Electra, and Nazimova, in spite of her Russian accent, which rings so strangely in Suffolk County, made so much of the sinning Clytemnestra that the drama lost much when she withdrew into the shades of the House of Mannon never to return. Earle Larimore, too, as Orin-Orestes, gave the rôle a human quality which could hardly have been expected in the writing, and Thomas Chalmers, with an opera-trained speaking voice, not only overcame the trick sound-currents of the theatre but gave a healthy robustness to the rather murky proceedings which was reassuring, as long as it lasted. Lee Baker, the first of a long string of entries to die, may have seemed a little stiff, but I suspect that it was a rather stiff part. In short, Philip Moeller in his direction, and the cast in their interpretation, and especially Mr. Jones in his settings, all did more than their share to raise Mr. O'Neill to the undisputed, and probably for a long time uncontested, eminence of the First Dramatist of Our Time. Not that he wasn't there already, but it is good to be sure.

But while we are on our feet, let us drink once again to the Count of Monte Cristo.

The New Yorker, November 7, 1931

QUESTIONNAIRE

D URING the Holy Week lull in the theatre several of the dramatic critics got into mischief and came out with questionnaires designed to test their readers' knowledge of the Drama. Even the mildest of such tests are always a humiliation to me, owing to a tendency (the last remnant of a college education) to say "Samuel J. Tilden" when I mean "Rutherford B. Hayes" or "aluminum" when I mean "chromium," thereby making it impossible for me to answer correcty even those questions to which I *know* the answer, to say nothing of the myriad of which I am ignorant.

But when a set of questions on the very subject at which I am supposed to be earning my living can throw me, then it passes humiliation and becomes a blind rage. When I find myself naming, with great facility, three of Pinero's plays in answer to "Name three plays of Clyde Fitch," then it is time to run head on into a stout wall and tear my clothes from my body. It is in such a mood that I have decided to salve my feelings by working up a questionnaire of my own, to which I *must* get the right answers because I work backward from answer to question. Even then I am afraid that I must watch myself. Here, then, is a test based on the theatrical season which is now drawing to a close, a test on which I shall rate 100 and nobody else can guess a single answer. That ought to make me feel better.

1. What three plays am I thinking of?

2. Name every character in "The Good Companions" and who played each in the New York engagement, and *don't skip*.

3. What have the following in common: Gilbert Miller; "The Count of Monte Cristo;" Fort Worth, Texas? Name them.

4. Who wrote Ravel's "Bolero" and what producer staged it at the Earl Carroll Theatre?

5. In what murder-mystery plays during the past season could the corpse be seen breathing?

6. How many representatives of the Younger Generation on the stage would you want to have as your own children? How many actually were?

7. What has George Spelvin in common?

8. What is George M. Cohan looking at when he keeps turning his head toward the wings? What is Ed Wynn looking at when *he* keeps turning his head toward the wings? Could they possibly be looking at each other?

9. What is this Sex they are all talking about?

10. In what crook plays during 1931-2 were the following phrases used: (1) "bumped off," (2) "take for a ride," (3) "you lousy bum, you"?

11. How do actors get down when they exit by running upstairs? Is there really a bedroom up there?

12. How does Edna Best eat a cracker at every performance of "There's Always Juliet" without taking a drink of water?

13. Name four playwrights who are cross at the critics.

14. What is in the suitcases which wives carry when they are prevented at the foot of the stairs from leaving home?

15. In what play does Florette, the Maid, appear?

16. Hum one number from a current musical without getting into some number which has been written before.

17. Jump through this.

18. Write a play by a Hungarian playwright. Write two plays by a Hungarian playwright.

19. Who were the following: (1) Eugene O'Neill, (2) Martin Luther, (3) Martin Beck?

20. Who wrote Mae West?

21. Name one play which closed solely because of bad notices. Name one play which kept running solely because of good notices. Name one play.

22. What are English actors saying?

23. What play that was consigned to the ashcan by this department ran until it was the oldest play on Broadway? (Oh, *not* "Abie's Irish Rose"! That wasn't in this department, we did not consign it to the ashcan, and we are sick of hearing about it. The play that we mean opened last fall.)

24. How many jokes does a musical comedy have to have before it is out of the "nice" class?

25. What trilogy by what famous playwright gave what pain in the neck?

26. Why is "playwright" spelled "playwright"?

27. What well-known scenic artist suffers from misplaced hyphen, and why won't people learn?

28. What theatre on Forty-ninth Street gives off the odor of burning honey?

29. What was the first couch in the modern theatre to be used for something besides sex? Is Alexander Woollcott really Duse?

30. Isn't this all getting a little tiresome?

The New Yorker, March 26, 1932

SHAVINGS FROM SHAW

R EVIEWING a play by Shaw is an ungrateful task at best, for, no matter what the reviewer may say, he must necessarily make himself out something of a whippersnapper. It is agreed, I suppose, that Shaw is a really Great Man, otherwise he could not, wearing a full beard, have his picture taken in a bathing suit (a test of greatness which even Napoleon could hardly have come through with complete success). It is also agreed, I hope, that anything that Shaw writes has distinction, not so much because it is always good, but because it is so much better than anything else of its kind. So either to praise or to pan Shaw must seem equally presumptuous on the part of a man who, even in his most luxuriant season, can raise only a fragment of a mustache.

Let us say then, in all humility, that "Too True to Be Good" is not Shaw at his best. It is not Shaw at his worst, for he has toyed with the movies like an elderly kitten with a ball of string, but it is rather as if the Great Irishman had forsaken his abstemiousness for one night and, under the mellowing influence of several rum punches, had indulged in the prerogative of all good stews, reminiscent and repetitious philosophizing. "Too True to Be Good" seems to be the work of someone who has been reading too much Shaw and has nothing to add to it—except, as the bun wears off, a despairing "Whatever is to become of us all?" Following the late lamented "A Night of Barrie" at the Playhouse, we have "A Night of Shaw" at the Guild. But don't think that you couldn't spend worse nights.

The slightly drunken and phantasmagorical nature of the proceedings is heightened by the structure, or lack of structure, of the piece and the heterogeneous makeup of the cast which has been assembled, with rare abandon on the part of the Guild, to act in it. It is like one of those dreams that one has in which Ludwig Lewisohn wins a sack race and a visit to the Aquarium at the Battery ends

135

one up in the Taj Mahal. "Then it seemed as if Bea Lillie came on, dressed in a sort of bathing suit, and talked with a British colonel, only it was on more of a mountain, and Hope Williams was there, having just got out of a great big bed somewhere near London and put on a Greek peasant's costume to chase her mother around a big rock labelled 'St. Paul's.' Then I woke up." This nightmare feeling of not knowing what in hell is going to happen next, together with the bright colors of Jonel Jorgulesco's settings, helps considerably to keep those heavy eyelids open and to lend a certain excitement which Mr. Shaw's reiterated views on vegetables, war, inoculation, and the British army could not possibly have furnished had the scene been laid in a drawing-room.

During the first, and very bad, act you think that maybe it was a mistake to put Miss Lillie in the part of the nurse, for her own (unfortunately not inimitable) comedy tricks threaten to eliminate Shaw entirely from the proceedings. But as the show wears on, it is Miss Lillie's personal comedy which makes the whole thing bearable, and the more she eliminates Shaw, the better you like it. It may be presumptuous to look askance at Shaw's philosophizing, but when he essays gags he lays himself open to comparison with the lowliest gagster, for a gag is a gag, whether it be pulled by George Bernard Shaw or Lou Holtz, and most of Mr. Shaw's gags are perfectly terrible. If Miss Lillie were not there to lend grace to them by a slight and regal inclination of the head or a convulsive dip into a candy box, matters in "Too True to Be Good" would be in a parlous state on many occasions. It may not be good Shaw, but neither is Shaw in this instance.

The rest of the cast, with the possible exception of Miss Williams, who needs a good scene by Philip Barry or Donald Ogden Stewart to fit her particularly immobile type of acting, do wonders with the old material at hand. Ernest Cossart as the Colonel, Leo G. Carroll as Private Meek, Frank Shannon as the evangelical sergeant, and Claude Rains as a strange man with an umbrella, all place Mr. Shaw greatly in their debt. But it is Hugh Sinclair, a young Englishman who has been doing some excellent acting in a very quiet way for some time (ever since he stopped playing Miss Lillie's accompaniments in vaudeville), who takes the one important thing that Shaw has to say and makes it seem ten times more important by his inspired reading of it as the final curtain comes down. I have never seen an audience stopped short in the midst of its hat-reaching as Mr. Sinclair stopped that opening-night audience at the Guild Theatre. Standing at the front of the stage, after dismissing the rest of the cast one by one in the manner of a finale to a Charlot revue, this young man, representing, it is to be supposed, Shaw himself, confesses the bankruptcy of the world in general and of himself in particular. "I am by nature and destiny a preacher. . . .But I have no Bible, no creed; the war has shot both out of my hands. . . .I stand midway between youth and age, like a man who has missed his train; too late for the last and too early for the next. What am I to do? What am I?" Here, for the first time, we see what Shaw has been saying in all this vaudeville. He has been throwing everything he has said before into a melting pot and the residue is dross, because, with the world's spiritual market as it stands today, it is unnegotiable. Whether it is what Shaw has written or the way in which Mr. Sinclair reads it, the fact remains that the final speech of "Too True to Be Good" is a thrilling, and rather terrifying, thing to hear. No more convincing proof of Shaw's real stature in the world today could be had than the panicky feeling which comes over you as you hear this despairing cry coming out from the gathering fog as the curtain falls. If this brave general admits defeat, then the army is indeed lost.

The New Yorker, April 16, 1932

CONFESSIONAL

MR. BARNUM is very wise always to bring his Circus into New York in mid-April, for a great many people would rather go to the Circus than to the mid-April theatrical openings. And you don't have to be very crazy about the Circus to feel that way, either.

I, myself, when it comes time to choose between the premières of plays called "Angeline Moves In" and the combined shows of Messrs. Barnum, Bailey, and Ringling, usually elect to stay at home among my books (pulling them out of the bookcases and throwing them on the floor). This is not because I do not think the Circus a more important event than "Angeline Moves In" but because I have a slight circus phobia which it would take no psychiatrist to diagnose. I was once very badly frightened by a circus.

It was when I was working on a newspaper, and, being not very good at getting facts which would hold the reader's attention and yet be libel-proof, had been shifted to the "Sunday department," where I did a page of man-about-town chitchat every Sunday. (I had just come to New York to work and so knew the town from stem to stern.) One week the Boss told me to go up and be a clown in the Circus for a night, and write twelve hundred words on it.

By a lucky coincidence, the press-agent of the Circus heard of the plan and offered his assistance in getting me into the ranks of the clowns. Mr. Buck Baker, who, I am happy to see, is still the dean of the fun-makers, took me into what is known as "tow," and I made my combination début and farewell tour as a clown in the old Madison Square Garden on April 20 let-me-see-when-was-it. We might as well face it right here at the start—I was *not* a success, even *d'estime*.

The process of getting painted-up was exciting, and those of my colleagues who helped me into a rather unpleasant pair of false feet proved to be charming companions; so I had no reason to feel that everything was not going to go much merrier than a marriage bell. And when Mr. Baker told me my first assignment, which was merely to sit still on the edge of a ring and fish from a pail, I had visions of making something of a name for myself. You can't go wrong just sitting on the edge of a ring and fishing from a pail—which is probably what was in Mr. Baker's mind, too.

This act went off so well, and the whole audience was so electrified by my artistry, that I was next put into an automobile with two other clowns, this time to drive around the arena backward. The whole thing was a hoax, really, for, although I *seemed* to be at the wheel, the real driver was hidden in back and the automobile was so constructed as to look as if it were going backward when, all the time, it was forging ahead. (This model has since been discontinued.)

Frankly, I did not like this. I was told to sit at the dummy wheel and simulate terror, but the terror was at least eight-tenths genuine, for I am not given to such antics in automobiles, as any taxi-driver in New York will tell you. I clutched the wheel in genuine apprehension and, when my mind functioned at all, it was to lay plans for getting the hell out of Madison Square Garden at the first available opportunity.

Having completed the circuit of the ring to the great delight of thousands of admirers, I was lifted out and taken to the ante-room. Here Mr. Baker outlined the next stunt.

"We get into this big bus," he said, "twelve of us. Then we start riding around the ring, clowning and making noises. When I give the signal, the bus explodes and breaks in two pieces and we all fall out. But I will give another signal first, which means that we are all to start jumping, for, if you wait until the bus really explodes, it will be just too bad. Remember now, when I give the *first* signal, JUMP!"

This seemed all very explicit, but not particularly attractive. Too much depended on jumping at just the right moment. I don't jump much under the best of conditions, and these conditions were certainly not among the best. Going around the ring backward had not tended to build up my morale, and I had an awful feeling that I might possibly crack if subjected to any more horrors—crack mentally and perhaps physically. As all this happened before prohibition, I did not drink, and so was dependent on what little courage I had of my own—which was not enough.

As soon as Mr. Baker's back was turned (if he sees this now, and remembers at all, I hope that he will forgive me), I found a stairway which led up into the famous tower of the old Garden and tried mounting it, three steps at a time. My false feet were not helpful, but terror gave me unwonted agility and I doubt if even the most dexterous acrobat could have caught me, once I got under way. It was quite a big tower, as my older readers will remember, and I was leaping upward and onward for quite a long time, but each leap took me farther and farther away from that bus, and I was content. I heard voices calling my name from below, and once, to my horror, someone started up toward the dressing-room after me, but, thank God, a circus, like the play, must go on, and by the time the big bus number was over, I had rushed down and taken off my makeup and was out in Madison Avenue, something in the spirit of a startled faun, with just a touch of yellow in its coloring. The next day I told the Boss that there wasn't any story in it—just the old stuff.

I have been to the Circus several times since, having had sons several times since, but each time that bus has come on and exploded, through some grim machination of Fate, right in front of my box (I get a free box, being a possible dispenser of publicity). And, if Mr. Fellowes doesn't mind, I am through going to any more circuses. I love the tang of the elephants, and I love the gay laughter of children, but, I am sorry, I cannot face Buck Baker and his boys in that bus again. I have been yellow many times since, but that was my first fall, and I had rather not be reminded of it.

All of this is to explain why, although I did not go to "Angeline Moves In" and Yasha Yushny's Russian vaudeville, "The Blue Bird," I also did not go to the Circus.

The New Yorker, April 30, 1932

TOP AND BOTTOM

I T IS usually a mistake to see an old favorite revived, especially if it be a musical comedy. You may have been going about for years mooning reminiscently to less experienced friends, letting a sad look come into your eyes when excerpts from the dear score are played, and muttering "They don't write 'em like that nowadays," until you actually believe yourself that "The Prince of Pilsen" or "The Yankee Consul" were the best shows you ever saw or ever expect to see.

And then, during a slow stretch, some manager revives your Old Favorite. The least that you can do is to take a theatre party including everyone to whom you have been touting it for fifteen or twenty years, and this you do with every confidence in the world. Then begin the explanations. It isn't done as well as it was originally—these shoddy revivals, you know. Something has been left out, presumably about two-thirds of the book. (What ever became of those laughs which followed on each other's heels, as you remember it?) The orchestra isn't big enough and they are not using the same orchestrations. And, above all, the people, those wonderful people of the original cast, are gone. Obviously *something* has happened.

"Show Boat" is just about the first Old Favorite to hold up in revival. Perhaps this is because it is not so old. Four and a half years would seem to be the ideal time to allow a musical-comedy hit to mellow. Possibly it is because Mr. Ziegfeld has revived it with just as much care as he first produced it, and with the original cast (with two exceptions which make it even better). Even though the prices are lower, there has been no perceptible scrimping on Mr. Ziegfeld's part. But probably it is because in "Show Boat" Jerome Kern and Oscar Hammerstein II wrote the best all-around musical comedy of modern times. Certainly the combination of these three factors makes it the best musical-comedy revival.

It seems even better in revival than it did on that opening night in Christmas Week of 1927, because Mr. Kern's lovely melodies have made just enough of a nook for themselves in our minds to fit in comfortably the first second we hear the opening bars. We also know, when Mr. Winninger crouches low and says "Hap—," that it is eventually to be followed by "—py New Year!" and we get that much longer laugh. We enjoy the opening scene on the levee all the more because we know that it is to be followed by an even better scene on the stage of the Cotton Blossom and that they both are to be followed by the scenes at the World's Fair and the Trocadero Music Hall. And when we look at our programs and see that the cast still includes Edna May Oliver (we hope that Miss Oliver realized, from the stirring greeting accorded to her on the opening night, that there are some things the theatre can give an actress that the movies can't, including the personal contact of a loving audience), Charles Winninger, Eva Puck and Sammy White, Helen Morgan, and Norma Terris, then we know exactly what to expect—and what is even more grateful, we get it. Dennis King, one of the two substitutions, although his speech is not so much that of one of the old Ravenals of Tennessee as one of the old Ravenals of Stoke Poges, is an added asset to the ensemble and it is hardly necessary to say that Paul Robeson makes "Old Man River" an even more thrilling experience than it was at first—which is saying just about as much as could be said without bursting a blood vessel.

Incidentally, we ought to know enough by now to remember that the first singing of "Old Man River" comes fairly early in the show and that no dinner party in the word is worth lingering over long enough to miss it. In fact, it would be a good idea to postpone dinner until midnight and get into the theatre for the rise of the curtain, for in 1928 a great many people never heard "Only Make Believe" at all until they heard it played around town or in Paris. Not since "Iolanthe" has there been a score which started off with so many prescribed numbers—and also finished with them. It would be an impertinence to list all the ones that you must hear, for you know them already, but in revival we also find that several of the songs accorded to Miss Puck and Mr. White, although never featured, have smart enough lyrics by Mr. Hammerstein to make them stand out in any ordinary show, especially as sung by Miss Puck and Mr. White. (Oh, let's drop all this pretence and call them "the Whites." Everybody knows about it by now.) And, once again, let us call attention to young Mr. Hammerstein's not-enough-recognized claim to distinction as a lyricist and librettist. Working with the original rich sentiment of Miss Ferber's novel, he has fashioned words in such a manner as not only to bear analysis but also to dig pretty deeply into the heart-strings for a succession of good ripe chords.

Perhaps some of the nostalgic quality of "Show Boat," unusual in a show which is not five years old, comes from the fact that when we first heard it we were having an awfully good time. (Remember 1928?) Public psychology being what it is, stranger things have happened than people going out of the present production of "Show Boat" sufficiently inspired to have an awfully good time again. Just as we used to wear the same green tie to examinations for good luck, it may be that what we needed was the sound of "Old Man River" to keep things going.

The New Yorker, May 28, 1932

THE OLD DAYS

IF YOU think that these are dull days in the theatre, just wait until they appear in somebody's reminiscences along about 1965 and you will realize that we are right at this moment living in the Golden Age, surrounded by lovable old characters and surfeited with plays which *are* plays and actors who *are* actors. (By 1965 it is hoped that some way will have been found to remedy this last condition.)

In a book probably to be called "Footlight Memories," you will be able to read of the good old days along Broadway in the early 'thirties and you will lay the book aside with those old eyes dimmed with tears and, crashing one of your grandchildren over the head, will murmur: "Tsk-tsk [some day I am going into a room by myself and try making that noise, those were the times when Titans strode the earth." And your grandchild, feigning indifference at the moment, will pick up the book after you have gone and will read something like the following:

Along about 1932, the American theatre was at the height of its glory and Broadway (as they called Forty-fifth Street then) was alive with glamorous men and women whose words and deeds would fill a book—in fact, *are* filling a book. I was a young man at the time, fresh and impressionable, and it was my high privilege to have met and known some of these characters, who are today almost legends in the annals of our stage. We shall not see their like again.

I remember an institution called the Actors' Dinner Club, which was the centre of the social life of the theatre at that time, and there one could drop in at any time of the day or night and be sure of meeting someone who was helping to write theatrical history by his very existence. It was along about '32 when this institution was at the height of its glory and, as I was at the time a press-agent for one of the big producers (Mr. Joe Zelli, who came over from Paris to set the town by the ears with his production of "Mr. Papavert"), I was naturally "in the know" and admitted to all the councils of the leaders. The press-agent in those days was the liaison officer between the Stage and Society and second in importance only to the producer himself. In fact, he sometimes *was* the producer.

It was at a rehearsal for the big musical-comedy success "Everybody's Welcome" at the old Shubert Theatre (the Shubert Theatre stood at one end of what was known as "Shubert Alley," a gay thoroughfare of the Rialto where the bloods of the day were wont to congregate and pass remarks which were one day to become a part of the country's literature) that I first met Cecil Lean. Cecil Lean was famous as the partner of Cleo Mayfield and vice versa, and one of the figures who had made American musical comedy the sensational factor in the cultural life of the times that it then was. The cast of "Everybody's Welcome" included such names as Oscar Shaw, Jack Sheehan, Roy Roberts, Spencer Barnes, Charles Garland, Edna Hedin, and Ann Pennington, and they were all on the stage rehearsing as I entered the theatre with Sam Zolotow, the critic of the *Times*. "There's Cecil Lean," Zolotow said to me, and I immediately asked if I could meet him. "I don't know why not," replied Zolotow, who was very powerful in the theatre during the early part of the century and could arrange a meeting with almost any of the stars if he happened to take a fancy to you. And so it was that I met Cecil Lean and learned from him that it looked as if "Everybody's Welcome" would be the sensation that it later turned out to be. I remember that he said at the time: "I think we've got something here," and he certainly was right. They did have something.

It was at about this time that Robert Sparks produced "Monkey," the mystery play which came into the Mansfield Theatre (I think it was the Mansfield, although it may have been the Biltmore, which was directly across the street).

Opening nights in those days were glamorous affairs and places in the pit were at a premium. Sometimes great crowds would congregate outside the theatre to see the notables as they entered, and hordes of autograph collectors would push their way forward to secure signatures which would one day make their little books precious items for historians. There was always Reuben, the delicatessen man, and Tammany Young, the Broadwayite *par excellence*, to say nothing of the critics, who would congregate on the curb between the acts to decide whether or not they would let the play live. "The Death Watch," they were called, and if one were bold enough, one might draw near to their little circle and overhear such remarks as "—so the girl said to the sailor—" or "I get mine usually right after eating." It was during these little sidewalk conferences that Kelcey Allen, the critic for *Women's Wear*, got off many of his quips, which would next day be all over town, attributed to "Frisco."

We of today, when our theatre seems sunk in commercialism, find it hard to believe that managers ever put on plays for the sheer love of the production, with never a thought of the money return. And yet, on looking over my old programs for 1930-32, I find any number of ventures which, even before they were brought into New York, must have been sure-fire failures, palpably so to the most inexperienced eye, plays which not only could never make a penny but stood to lose hundreds and hundreds of dollars. Only men who love the Theatre for itself could have subjected themselves to such beatings in its name.

One might run on like this forever, recalling names and faces, plays and music, all of which have long since passed into the records of the great days of the American Theatre. I do not feel, as many do, that the theatre today in 1965 is definitely decadent, and that the bloom of the early 'thirties is lost forever. It will return, I am sure. But before it can return, we must breed another race like that which stalked Broadway in the old days, a race of actors and playwrights, producers and critics, who faced life with integrity, "gentlemen unafraid."

The New Yorker, July 2, 1932

THE LETTER-BOX

EVERY once in a while this department wakes up in the middle of the night in a cold sweat thinking of how little it really gives its readers in the matter of cultural dialectics. No stimulating discussions on the Theory of Acting ever seem to arise from the opinions printed on this page, and Sir Henry Irving or the team of Beaumont and Fletcher might as well have been civil engineers for all the attention they ever get under our all-too-parochial heading, "The Theatre." The only letters that we inspire are so specific as to be strictly personal and run in much the same vein from year to year: "You dumb cluck, you—don't you know a good show when you see one?" or "Where do you get off to call yourself a dramatic critic, you Algonquin log-roller!" Arguments like this (if there *is* any argument) cannot really be said to constitute an Open Forum.

The dramatic editors of London papers sometimes give their entire columns over to heated discussions of whether an actor should *feel* what he is acting or only *think* it, and the words "subjective" and "objective" are as common in their pages as "swell" and "punko" are in these. Of course, perhaps the fact that we have no very decided opinions of our own on these matters may have something to do with it, but there also must be a definite lack of class to the whole department to leave our readers as cold as it seems to. It is very discouraging.

In lieu of controversial contributions on the subject of the Art of the Theatre, we have resorted to the well-known columnar subterfuge of writing some of our own and signing other people's names to them, in the hope that we may start something which will relieve our selfconsciousness of being merely a topical compendium of journalistic jottings on "Today on Broadway." There is also the practical consideration that if we relied on "Today on Broadway," there would be nothing to jot.

A.J.L. writes from Boston: "Your remarks on the real province of scenic design in the delineation of character seem to me to err on the side of horsefeathers. If, as you

147

say, the actor should always remain hidden behind some piece of scenery, with only a hand or a foot showing, what, then, becomes of your costumer? We know that in the days of Shakespeare, and well on into the Restoration drama, the rôles of women were played by boys and those of boys were played by women (thus accounting for the theory held in many quarters that Shakespeare himself was really Ann Hathaway), but, as Shelbourne has pointed out in his 'Use and Abuse of the Hautboy in Elizabethan England,' the costumes of the time were designed to *emphasize* rather than *minimize* the essential grotesquerie of the system and to produce an effect which, given a certain tempo of scenic design, would—where was I? Oh, yes! If, then, the actor is never to appear, why dress him at all?"

From "Scrutator," in Atlanta, Ga., comes the following objection to our article on "Meals on the Stage": "I cannot agree with you that real food should be used in scenes which depict eating at table. It is quite true that, with a real mouthful of steak-and-kidney pie, the actor might have so much trouble in swallowing that he would be unable to repeat the lines or even might choke to death, but would the benefit resulting from this make up for the lengthening of the running time of the piece? The great Coquelin, in his book 'L'Art du Comédien says: "Il suit de là que le comédien doit être double. Il a son *un*, qui est l'instrumentiste; son *deux*, qui est l'instrument. Le *un* conçoit le personnage à créer, ou plutôt, car la conception appartient à l'auteur, il le voit tel que l'auteur l'a posé: c'est Tartuffe, c'est Hamlet, c'est Arnolphe, c'est Roméo; et ce modèle, le *deux* le réalise.' Does this make my point, or doesn't it?"

(We cannot refrain from pointing out to "Scrutator" that the great Coquelin, in the same work, also went on to say: "Il est faux, il est ridicule, de penser que le comble de l'art soit pour le comédien d'oublier qu'il est devant le public." *Touché*, "Scrutator"?)

"The question," writes Leo G. Garm, of San Francisco, "of whether or not the curtain should be raised at all during the playing of Restoration drama is a vexing one. In the days of Congreve and Vanbrugh the theory unquestionably was that the curtain *should* be raised, in order that the audience might see and hear what was going on. Today, however, there is some doubt as to the necessity for this. Those who attend a Restoration comedy *know* what is going on, otherwise they would not be there (or perhaps they are there because they do *not* know what is going on, in which case they are better off with the curtain down). In either case, keeping the curtain lowered throughout the entire play can do no harm."

What do *you* think on these subjects, readers of this department? Come on—for Heaven's sake, let's get some life into this thing!

The New Yorker, July 9, 1932

"DESIGN FOR LIVING"

M R. NOEL COWARD'S design for living, as set forth in his play of that name, is an extremely freehand drawing of delightful line and aspect, regardless of its practicability as a blueprint. (And who is to say whether it is practical or not?) We may wonder a little just what would happen in a possible fourth act, after the two young men and the one young woman have gone back to living together again. We may speculate over the housing scheme and try to figure out just who would get whom, and what the *tertium quid* would do during those long spring evenings in Paris. (And stranger things have happened than that it should turn out to be the young lady who was out of luck.)

But, whatever goes on after the play has ended, there is one thing certain while it is going on: everyone, including the Messrs. Coward and Lunt, Miss Fontanne, and the audience itself, has been having a simply *marvelous* time of it.

In its light and airy way, "Design for Living" tinkles delicately at a more or less revolutionary note in human relationships. Revolutionary for the theatre, that is. When we stop to think of it, we realize that Mr. Coward has relegated that little imp Dan Cupid (at least in his more brutish moods) to a place among the minor prophets and has made him something of a nuisance into the bargain. Sex, as we were taught it in Sunday School, is seen as a "small enchantment," something which intrudes itself, like a charming but drunken friend who rings up at four A.M. for a party, spoiling the well-ordered routine of three people who would otherwise have been having a perfectly good time just fooling around together. Perhaps those long spring evenings in Paris do not hold so much treachery after all, provided the two young men have learned their lesson. But Miss Fontanne must give up wearing those yellow negligees if the thing is ever to work out properly.

That Mr. Coward has been told quite enough about the quality of his own dialogue is shown in the scene in which his playwright hero reads aloud the newspaper reviews of his latest success. "Witty," "provocative," "polished," "nay, even brilliant" are words which apparently irk Mr. Coward by now, especially when used in conjunction with the qualifying adjective "thin." (He forgot "brittle.") But the fact remains that his dialogue *is* witty, provocative, polished, nay, even brilliant. Even dearer to this reviewer than the "brittle" quips are the little words and phrases used in quite matter-of-fact connections, chosen as evidently only an Englishman can choose words and used here as only Mr. Coward among Englishmen can use them. "Squirming with archness," as Miss Fontanne describes herself in her fine speech in the first act. Brandy "hurtling down" on astonished insides. "You must be here to lash me with gay witticisms." And, to me one of the funniest lines in the play, when the neophyte maid is unable to find anyone at the other end of the telephone after a long barrage of "'Allo"s and Mr. Coward says: "Never mind, Mrs. Hodge. We mustn't hope for too much at first." It is all very discouraging to one who has a working vocabulary of eighteen words, six of them being "swell" and "lousy."

There is, in fact, almost a plethora of amusing lines in "Design for Living." The outstanding ones in several of the scenes would be even more outstanding if some of the lesser ones were cut. Even the incomparable drinking scene, in which Messrs. Coward and Lunt destroy a whole quart of brandy, with chasers from the sherry bottle ("real old Armadildo"), without once descending into the sordid routine of such scenes—even this could be cut to advantage, although I do not want to be the one to decide what should be cut. The lines should not be thrown away, but wrapped up in tissue paper and saved for another comedy. "Design for Living" just doesn't need them, that's all.

But who are we, in this day and age, to cavil at too much of a good thing, when good things are so scarce? And who are we to feel vaguely uncomfortable at Mr. Coward's third act and final curtain, as if three people whom we had learned to like very much had suddenly gone slightly bad on us? (The decision they came to was logical and right enough, but it seemed as if they might have gone about it with a little less ruthless touch, considering that they were such pleasant people really.)

These quibblings are more or less beside the point when we consider that Mr. Coward has not only given us himself, Miss Fontanne, and Mr. Lunt at their very best (I didn't like the character of Gilda very much, what with her intolerance of success and comfortable hotels, but Miss Fontanne made everything all right) but has also supplied us with food for thought and an evening of practically uninterrupted delight.

The New Yorker, February 4, 1933

"THE 3-PENNY OPERA"

EVERYTHING looked so rosy for a good report card this week that Teacher is almost tempted to make believe that he liked "For Services Rendered" and "The 3-Penny Opera" better than he did, just to keep your spirits up. Certainly a schedule containing a new play by Somerset Maugham and a highly publicized revival of "The Beggar's Opera" with modern German fixings ought to have turned out more excitingly than it did. As it was, we are almost exactly where we were before.

"The 3-Penny Opera" did leave us with a little something of value, if only the haunting score of Kurt Weill. Although it is modernistic German music, it has moments of strange sweetness which most modernistic composers fight like demons to avoid, and one or two numbers you would almost swear were written to please the ear instead of confusing it. It has new rhythms, and fascinating ones, but withal a recollection of the old sentimental ballads which used to be thrown on a screen for community singing. I can't figure it out.

There is also a cockeyed amorphous quality about the production which is amusing for a little while until you see that great pride is being taken in it. You are interested, chiefly because you don't see what the hell they are up to. The general effect is that of a show being put on by amateurs in Fortnum & Mason's window, where tweed coats and sport sweaters lie draped about jars of greengages and Yorkshire pies just as if it were the most natural juxtaposition in the world.

Although the scene changes from the stables of the Duke of Devonshire to a beggars' establishment in Soho, and from there to a homelike bordel and the Old Bailey, there is always a tremendous pipe organ in the background and the imminence of old clothes racks and stereopticon screens in the shadows of the flies. It is safe to say that you never saw anything like it before—and may never again.

This strange dream quality of the setting and the score is unfortunately dissipated during the reading of the lines, although there is plenty of confusion as to the period. Modern idioms are thrown in, with not particulary comic effect, with a great deal that must be genuine Queen Anne humor because it is so dull. The costumes, on the other hand, represent humanity at some period of its development in the nineteenth century, presumably around the time of the Reform Act in England, although we can be sure of nothing except that the coronation of a queen was impending. In addition to all this, the German author, Herr Bert Brecht (at present dignified by Herr Hitler's disapproval), has thrown in a great deal of sociological and political satire which may have been delicious stuff in the original German of the "Dreigroschenoper" but in its English adaptation is only mildly important. And, having been one of the milder enthusiasts for the original work of John Gay (go ahead and shoot me!), I started with a severe handicap for an appreciation of the elements of the present work. In other words, I was just a bit teepy during long stretches of "The 3-Penny Opera."

The cast is a large one and decidedly uneven in quality. A pretty young lady named Steffi Duna, imported from Hungary by way of London, ought by all means to be seen again, although not, perhaps, as Polly Peachum. Robert Chisholm sings well and loudly as the hero, and Rex Weber at least gives Jonathan Peachum the benefit of his burlesque experience to the extent of making him the only one who knew definitely what he was about, whether you liked what he was about or not. I suppose that Rex Evans was meant to seem what he seems, which makes the character of "Tiger" Brown an amusing one in theory, anyway, and Josephine Huston has one song which is naughty enough to counteract its being a soprano solo.

It was good of Messrs. Krimsky and Cochran to take so much pains with "The 3-Penny Opera" and you probably will want to say you have seen it, as it is sure to be talked about in one way or another. Personally, I didn't have nearly as thin a time at it as some seem to have had, and would even recommend it to a select circle of friends who wouldn't hold it against me if they were bored a little while seeing and hearing something different.

Mr. Maugham, in "For Services Rendered," is very bitter and angry about the War, but so are a lot of people. If he had stuck to one or two, or even four or five, examples of the havoc that war can bring to one family, he might have made his point with a little less burlesque effect, but when blindness, insanity, sex-starvation, suicide, cashing phony checks, and even cancer in a dear old mother are thrown in one after the other as debits to be answered for by the war lords, we begin to feel, as we felt of "Dangerous Corner" and "We, the People," that if one more disclosure of sin and suffering is piled on, the thing will become ridiculous and somebody is going to laugh.

As I remember the English reviews when "For Services Rendered" opened in London, they didn't like it because it was too gloomy. That made me want to like it when it came here, for people who think that playwrights shouldn't be gloomy about the war are usually in the wrong about everything. But I am afraid that I see what they meant in this case. Mr. Maugham hasn't been gloomy so much as hog-wild. One is almost tempted to say: "*No* war could be as mean to one family as all that," and, before you know it, that sort of talk gets you into another war.

Whatever Mr. Sam Harris was thinking about when he brought "For Services Rendered" over here, he certainly did the right thing by it in casting. Fay Bainter, Jean Adair, Leo G. Carrol, Elizabeth Risdon, Jane Wyatt, and other names which give the seasoned playgoer a feeling of security when he sees them on the program, all have been oppressed with a load of war's horrors and each comes through with great credit and does what in wartime was known as his "bit."

Incidentally, the little old wartime "bit" that we each were to do has turned out to be quite a big boy now, hasn't it?

Somebody forgot to tell us when to stop doing it.

The New Yorker, April 22, 1933

"NIGHT AND DAY"

THE SONG "Night and Day" continues to thrive on its own merits and because Freddie Astaire refused to believe the obituary notices of "Gay Divorce," the show in which it is featured.

You must know that Mr. Cole Porter, lyricist of "Night and Day," shares the mantle of W. S. Gilbert with Ira Gershwin, Lorenz Hart, Irving Caesar, Irving Berlin, Joseph V. McKee, Howard Dietz, Bert Kalmar, George M. Cohan, Gus Kahn, Primo Carnera, and George Herman (Columbia Lou) Gehrig. Well, it seems to me that in this number, Mr. Porter not only makes a monkey of his contemporaries but shows up Gilbert himself as a seventh-rate Gertrude Stein, and he does it all with one couplet, held back till late in the refrain and then delivered as a final, convincing sock in the ear, an ear already flopping from the sheer magnificence of the lines that have preceded. I reprint the couplet:

Night and day under the hide of me
There's an Oh, such a hungry yearning,
   burning inside of me.

So what? Well, I have heard the song only by radio, and those whom I have heard repeat the refrain have sung that immortal couplet the same both times. Fortunate friends who have seen "Gay Divorce" report that the number is generously encored and reprised, and as a matter of course, most of the encores are pedal, not vocal. When they are vocal, the words are not changed.

Again, so what? Well, just as the apparently perfect lines in Allie Wrubel's song "As You Desire Me" courted attempts at improvement, so did this superb couplet of Mr. Porter's, and though the attempt is as much of a failure as the others, the fact that the song is still being sung on stage and air encourages me to publish a few modifications to which Freddie and the radio artists are welcome if ever they tire of the original.

This time my own kiddies were left out of the conference, most of them being away at school, taking a course in cuts. A little niece of mine, Miss Ann (Jake the Barber) Tobin of Niles, Mich., was the only party consulted. We agreed that there must be no needless trifling with the impeccable five words—"There's an Oh, such a"—which begin the second line; they should stand as written except where our rhythm made changes imperative.

Well, then, here is the first variant from Little Ann's pen, with spelling corrected by uncle:

Night and day under the rind of me
There's an Oh, such a zeal for spooning,
    ru'ning the mind of me.

And another, wherein she lapses into the patois:

Night and day under the peel o' me
There's a hert that will dree if ye think
    aucht but a' weel o' me.

And now a few by uncle himself:

1. Night and day under the fleece of me
    There's an Oh, such a flaming furneth
        burneth the grease of me.
2. Night and day under the bark of me
    There's an Oh, such a mob of microbes
        making a park of me.
3. Night and day under my dermis, dear,
    There's a spot just as hot as coffee
        kept in a thermos, dear.
4. Night and day under my cuticle
    There's a love all for you so true it
        never would do to kill.
5. Night and day under my tegument
    There's a voice telling me I'm he, the
        good little egg you meant.

The New Yorker, May 6, 1933

(*Editor's note*: We have to be a spoilsport and point out that the line which inspired these high-jinks is actually "Day and night under the hide of me. . .", not "Night and day. . ." Sorry.)

156

SUMMING UP

T HIS DEPARTMENT (the Department of Plant & Structures, in case you
have forgotten) would have issued its annual summary of the past
theatrical season a long time ago if it had not been for the fact that nobody
quite knew when the season was over. It might have been over almost any minute
after its opening in September, 1932. But strange people kept on giving shows,
and other strange people (a *few* others) kept going to them, and before we knew it,
June was just around the corner. (By the way, whatever became of June after she
divorced Lord Inverclyde?)

So, basing our deductions solely on the calendar, the Theatrical Season of
1932-33 should be over. But the difference between the Season *finie* and the
Season *en fleur* is so slight as to make one wonder if Pirandello wasn't right, after
all. Aren't we (pronounced "are-rent we") really just what we think we are? If we
think the Season is over, isn't it over? And mightn't this really be the Season from
now on, if we think it is? Oh well, let's not get gloomy, just before Memorial Day!

As some of you Seniors will remember, it has been our custom to review the
past theatrical year and predict the coming one, with a rather cynical summary of
the number of times an old gentleman in an ascot tie has said: "I remember your
mother, my dear, when she was as beautiful as you are," or the number of times
we may expect a runaway wife to be stopped at the foot of the stairs with her
traveling case in hand and to turn back, at the fall of the curtain, to try the whole
horrid business over again. We have made up purely arbitrary statistics, such as
that 482 characters in speakeasy scenes ordered 869 Old-Fashioneds and left them
only half-consumed because of the vile cold tea provided by the property man in
lieu of rye, and we have predicted that, during the coming year, 64 revue sketches
will black-out with the cuckold husband knocking on the closet door and saying
"Goodbye, Bill!" or some variant of that original masterpiece.

157

In short, this type of summary has become such a routine that a cynical reader might almost get up one for himself, with the payoff: "During the season 1933-34 there will be 47 lists made by commentators predicting that 46 comedy characters will say 'Oh, sure!' 486 times."

The only reason I am not doing the same thing this year is that it has been done, for all time and with staggering completeness, by Mr. George Jean Nathan in his latest book, "Since Ibsen." The boyish Dean of the Death Watch has made the rest of us dilettantes seem like pikers with one hundred and sixty-three pages of dramatic clichés which cover practically every ham situation or line of dialogue that has irritated professional playgoers since Shaw. The jig is up, as far as we are concerned.

One of the remarkable things about Mr. Nathan's book, aside from the incredible industry involved in setting it all down on paper, is the *tour de force* of memory which it represents. Any minor efforts in the same field which I have been able to get printed have been the result of assiduous and astigmatic pencilings on the margins of programs in the semi-dark of the theatre, pencilings which have resulted, as often as not, in indecipherable jumbles of words across each other or an intermingling of my own handwriting with the type of "What the Man Will Wear." The amount of valuable criticism of the Drama which has been lost to posterity through my inability to read it myself the next morning would fill a book as large, though not as astute, as Mr. Nathan's.

And yet, having dozed in the general vicinity of Mr. Nathan in every theatre in New York for the past ten years, I can swear that he never takes notes. I have even tried to borrow a pencil of him for my own cribbing and have found that he had none. He has sat very straight upright (as long as he has sat) and, aside from an occasional yawn or a peep through his fingers as if he held a pair of imaginary opera glasses (I have never beem able to figure out what he was up to in this maneuver and have tried it myself, succeeding only in blinding myself completely), he has given no indication of registering anything that was going on behind the footlights, except as material for immediate elimination.

And yet somethwere in the back of that curly head every line that he has heard has made its impression, including "But I can't go on like this, Ma—I don't know why—but I can't—sometimes I feel like I'm stifling!" and "You secured the option on those lots of land belonging to old Mrs. Waxbaum knowing that the railroad was coming this way."

But there is no way to quote from "Since Ibsen" without quoting the whole book. It is a monumental work which should have the effect of putting an end to playwriting—and to dramatic criticism, gosh darn it! It certainly has put an end to the type of article which annually appeared on this page at this season. I hope Mr. Nathan is satisfied.

The New Yorker, May 27, 1933

JUST "ROBERTA"

IN ORDER to get the full emotional value out of one of Jerome Kern's lovely scores, it really should be taken in a large, blue bowl of Oscar Hammerstein's special brew of sentimental ambrosia, as in "Music in the Air" or "Show Boat." It does not tear you down so much in a setting of gowns and gags like "Roberta." Sweet as the strains are when they strike the ear, the heart remains practically untouched.

"Roberta" (out of Alice Duer Miller's novel, "Gowns by Roberta") is a colorful and expensive pageant, with several other things aside from Mr. Kern's music to recommend it, including an agreeable cast. But it must also be said that it contains volley after volley of some of the most immature gags ever conceived by an adult mind. (I take it for granted that they are the product of an adult mind. No child could have had the stamina to stay up as late at rehearsals as must have been necessary in the fight to keep them in.)

This is too bad, because one is tempted, in reporting on the show to inquiring friends, to quote freely from the book before saying anything about the music, the settings, or the people concerned. Word-of-mouth advertising being what it is, the news value of "Roberta" does not seem to lie so much in the fact that Lyda Roberti is swell (or perhaps this has ceased to be news), that Fay Templeton steals the first scene, or that a new quipster of the Baker-Bernie school has been introduced in the person of Bob Hope, as that someone says: "She has given me the air," and someone else says: "Oh, I thought you said she had given you *an heir*!," or that another unfortunate says: "Underneath, she has a heart that's gold" (you have to say *"that's* gold" in order to get the full value out of the comeback), and someone comes back with: "Did you say 'gold' or 'cold'?" It is news like this that hurts a show.

It is especially unfortunate that "Roberta" is loaded to the gunwales with this type of freight, for there are several people in the cast who might very well do wonders with a really good crack. A comparative newcomer to Broadway, the aforementioned Bob Hope, has a slick, humorous style of delivery which ought to put him in the front rank of talking bandmasters as soon as he gets something to say which does not bring the blush of shame to his cheeks. George Murphy, besides dancing nicely, can make you think that his lines are almost good until you stop to mull them over. And, of course, Lyda Roberti *makes* her lines good, whether they are or not.

We might as well face the fact that Miss Roberti is what is known in scientific circles as an "irresistible force." It is practically impossible not to give in to her in the face of that disarming Polish grin. It is she who puts an end, for all time, to the dignity of silks and satins, when, following an elaborate fashion parade of Kiviette creations, she descends the steps dressed in royal bride's array, followed by train-bearers and bridesmaids, and destroys both the God of Love and the God of Fashion with a song called "I'll Be Hard to Handle," of which two lines are: "I'll say with a shrug, I think you're a mugg—to marry me." After this, we may expect no more bridal numbers.

It was a stroke of genius on someone's part to engage Miss Fay Templeton for the rôle of Roberta, for while she is on, the natural sentimentality surrounding her return to the musical-comedy stage supplies the missing heartbeats to Mr. Kern's music. During the offstage rendition of Russell Bennett's delicate arrangement of "The Touch of Your Hand," while Tamara and William Hain were wrapping her shawl about the old lady for her last nap, the best of the sweetness of "Music in the Air" was recaptured.

Tamara and Mr. Hain sing well together, and Tamara herself makes as nice a heroine as Mr. Kern could ask. A pretty tribute to the newly recognized Soviet Republic came in the last act when she, as an expatriate Russian princess, stood in full regalia and sang the Czarist national hymn. If Mr. Litvinoff happened to be celebrating the evening of his diplomatic *coup* by attending the opening of "Roberta," were his ears red!

Of the remaining principals, Mr. Raymond Middleton had the dual disadvantage of having to play a moronic fullback turned dressmaker and of not being asked to sing oftener.

Thus we see that "Roberta" has plenty of good points and that it is only because its bad points are so distracting that it turns out to be one of those praiseworthy musical comedies during which one is constantly looking at one's program to see how much more of it there is going to be.

The New Yorker, November 25, 1933

"THE LAKE" AT LAST

I F "THE LAKE" could have been brought into town like any other play, without all traffic having to be stopped for a two minutes' silence at noon on the day of its opening, it would have passed for what it is—a delicate little tragedy, well above the average in concept and writing, and something that you certainly should see if you are at all tender about the theatre. Nothing terribly important, but, like "The Faithful Heart," one of those unpretentious plays which you remember vaguely through the years as having once warmed you.

If, also, Miss Katharine Hepburn could have been smuggled into the lead direct from her understudying Miss Hope Williams in "Holiday," she would certainly have been hailed as a young actress with great promise. Not a great actress, by any manner of means, but one with a certain distinction which, with training, might possibly take the place of great acting in an emergency.

Just who was responsible for the advance heaving and panting which preceded "The Lake" and Miss Hepburn to Broadway it is difficult to say. I rather imagine that it was one of those spontaneous epilepsies which the public works itself into without outside aid, and which are so unfair to the objects, who may, or may not, consider themselves competent to live up to expectations.

Certainly the whole thing was based on Miss Hepburn's—I think the word is "meteoric"—success in the movies, and it is high time that it was understood that acting in the movies is not the same thing as acting on the stage. Depicting a character in short "takes" of one or two minutes each, with "retakes" if it does not work out right and no necessity of learning more than five speeches at a time, is considerably different from carrying a rôle through a whole play, with your one performance your final one. Photographing as beautifully as Miss Hepburn does, and being naturally intelligent (which is where she has the drop on many of her competitors in Hollywood), it is small wonder that she has become the young phenomenon of the screen. It was almost cruel to foist her into stardom on the stage with only these qualifications, and her poise, to carry her through.

It was even more cruel to place her in the position of being "supported" by two such trained and experienced actresses as Blanche Bates and Frances Starr. These two, leading ladies in their own right, behaved beautifully about the whole thing and did nothing that they might well have done to take the play right out of Miss Hepburn's hands and swing it along by themselves, but, in spite of their obvious determination to play fair, that is exactly what they did. I don't see how anyone could have thought that it would be otherwise. A play with both Blanche Bates and Frances Starr in it is an event in itself, and to place them in a supporting cast with subordinate billing to a young lady from the movies, however distinguished, was almost an affront to the theatre-going public. However, as they both were at their best, and had, in addition, most of the best lines in the play, the theatre-going public had the satisfaction of seeing the home team win. Mr. Colin Clive, also representing the actors' contingent, helped to prove that, after all, stage experience is an asset in putting on a show behind the footlights. He had the misfortune to be drowned in the second act, and to have to carry a busby at his own wedding, but, aside from these handicaps, he and Mr. Lionel Pape made a formidable team, with the Misses Bates and Starr, to carry "The Lake" into eminence.

The play itself, which was written by the late Dorothy Massingham and Murray MacDonald and had considerable success in London last season, more or less runs neck and neck with Miss Hepburn in quality. The first act, in which she is very good, is also very good, and at the final curtain one is convinced that something even better is in store from both sources. The young lady who becomes engaged to a man she does not love to get herself out of an ominous affair with a married man is a character whose future is of considerable interest, especially as everyone concerned, including the authors, appears to be deserving of civilized consideration. The second act, which contains an interlude of comedy during a wedding reception held in a rain-drenched marquee, followed by stark tragedy when the fugitive bridal couple skid into the lake, reached its high point, just as Miss Hepburn does, in the scene where she realizes that she really loves her substitute husband. Both Miss Hepburn and Mr. Clive are splendid here.

It is in the third act that the test for both the play and star comes, and both are disappointing. The play takes on a spurious Norwegian atmosphere, with a great deal of looking offstage at the lake and mooning about, ending nowhere. I do not mind a play's ending nowhere; in fact, I rather like it, as it flatters one into thinking that one can finish it for oneself. But "The Lake," in spite of its air of great significance during its final scenes, fails to be significant. It just peters out.

Miss Hepburn does not peter out along with the play, but she does show that she has a great deal to learn about acting. She gives a great deal of what she has got to the part, but it is just not enough. Here we have not the relief of closeups and long shots to give the effect of variety. We have a young actress with a rather monotonous delivery playing at being Duse. And the final curtain comes down with nobody being anything much.

The New Yorker, January 6, 1934

GOOD NEWS

T WELVE years ago this month, first-nighters, distributed in unexpectant attitudes around Maxine Elliott's Theatre, gradually found themselves straightening up and cupping their ears. Something was happening on the stage that they had not looked for. One of the decade's most dramatic pieces was being unfolded, without so much as a word of warning. As our own Nero would say, "And that play was called 'Rain'!"

It is a compensation for routine first-nighting that one always stands a chance of experiencing, at unexpected intervals, the thrill of gradual discovery that what is going on up there behind the footlights is the very thing that one has been going to the theatre hoping to see.

It usually begins with the realization that one has been sitting in the same position for twenty minutes without knowing it, head cocked uncomfortably on one side and feet pressed firmly against the floor. Then comes the excitement of being present in an absolutely silent audience. Finally the whole truth dawns. This is it!

For the second time in Maxine Elliott's Theatre, we experienced this excitement when, last week, "The Children's Hour" came in, without one initial fanfare, and quietly set itself up as the season's dramatic high-water mark. Along toward the end, it turned out to have its flaws, but they were flaws of overproduction rather than of quality. It has two too many endings, any one of which would have sufficed.

In "The Children's Hour," Miss Lillian Hellman has written a fine, brave play, and has written it cleanly and, up until the last quarter, so tightly that there is not one second when you can let your attention wander, even if you wanted to.

It tells a story which would have been impossible of telling in public in the days when "Rain" was considered daring and "The Captive" was being banned by the police. A monster of child, a pupil in a girls' school, deliberately concocts a malicious tale of Lesbian relations between the two young head-mistresses, with the result that their school is broken up, their lives ruined, and one of them driven to suicide. Their suit for libel against the girl's grandmother, who spreads the lie, is dismissed, and the young woman who is left to face the world does so alone without even the refuge of the marriage which she had planned.

The language is frank, franker than we have yet had on the subject, but it is immaculate. I doubt if there will be any giggling, even at nervous matinées. Certainly there can be no offence to the adult mind. On the contrary, the effect should be highly salutary in the horror aroused at the enormity of irresponsible slander in such matters.

Aside from several minor objections toward the end, such as the one that the engaged young woman made it a little unnecessarily hard for herself by sending her fiancé away, and that of the almost O'Neill piling up of tragedy on what was tragedy enough already, there might also be a feeling that such a dire situation would be faintly impossible, and that a young child of such obviously pathological deviltry could not gain credence in a court of law, unsupported by reputable evidence.

In case this worries you, it may be pointed out that Miss Hellman has court records to substantiate her story, records on which she must have based it, so identical are the main circumstances.

In Edinburgh, in 1810, two schoolmistresses, the Misses Woods and Pirie, were similarly accused by a girl pupil, who have even less to recommend her than the young villainess of Miss Hellman's play. A suit for slander was instituted (and, by the way, shouldn't this one have been for slander instead of libel? It was all done by word of mouth) against the girl's grandmother, and after ten years of losing, appealing, winning, appealing, and endless legal haggling, with no evidence other than that of the already discredited viper, the case came finally before the august House of Lords. Here a technical verdict was awarded the schoolmistresses, but further legal haggling set in and there is no record of their even having received a shilling for their ruined lives.

So, to doubters, Miss Hellman may offer as evidence (as she already must know) pages 111-146 of a reputable volume called "Bad Companions," by William Roughead, published in 1931 by Duffield & Green. Or even just point to Tom Mooney.

In producing "The Children's Hour," Mr. Herman Shumlin has shown not only courage but a fine sense of casting and direction (it is a marvellous job of direction he

167

has done). As the two unfortunate teachers, Katherine Emery and Anne Revere lend a credibility and dignity which are indispensable. Katherine Emmet plays the grandmother with just the right contrast of patrician righteousness and eventual humility, and Robert Keith, as the sole, unhappy male, has never been so convincing. The school children are all good, especially Barbara Beals as the tortured stooge for the young hell-cat, and no greater compliment could be paid to the amazing performance of Florence McGee than to say that at times the impulse is almost irresistible to leap upon the stage and strangle her. Our one regret is that we are denied the sight of her humiliation.

"The Children's Hour" is possibly not for the children, but for any grownup with half a mind, it is almost obligatory.

The musical shows are slow in coming in, but when they do come, they come good. "Anything Goes" was worth waiting for. Mr. Vinton Freedley has what might be called a "honey" on his hands at the Alvin, and things around town seem brighter than ever because of it.

He has taken the precaution of enlisting the services of several people who seem unable to displease the public. If there is anyone who does not love Victor Moore, he has the good sense to lie low. Mr. Moore is about the only comedian we know who is 100 per cent sure of his laugh, no matter what he says. As "Public Enemy No. 13" in the present opera (he is shattered when he learns that the government has finally dropped him entirely from the Public Enemy list as being too harmless. "I don't understand the present administration," he complains), we have Mr. Moore at the peak of his pathos.

William Gaxton, too, seems to be pretty well established as a sure bet, and it is difficult to decide whether people have a good time watching him because he himself seems to be having a good time, or vice versa. Anyway, everbody has a good time.

To complete his trio of safe plays, Mr. Freedley, who used to be a quarterback himself, has sent Miss Ethel Merman around the end into what is evidently an open field. Enough of Miss Merman is what people do not seem to get, and while I could wish that sometime soon she might be sent on without an evangelical "Hallelujah" number, I never let it interfere with my general appreciation of her talents.

Miss Bettina Hall has always exerted a good influence over me, and never more than here, for I do not quite believe her when she sings that she has a touch of the gipsy in her. She is an excellent antidote for the crass, bestial man-about-town influence of Mr. Moore.

Any show which has Cole Porter writing its music and lyrics need hardly try out in the provinces. Mr. Porter is in a class by himself, and by "class" is meant "class." In "You're the Top," he has exceeded even himself as a writer of original lyrics, and unless I do not know my theatregoers, the town will shortly be driving itself crazy trying to memorize the sequence of items indicating "Top." In this one song, he has summarized American Civilization better than any symposium of National Thinkers has ever been able to do.

The book was originally by Guy Bolton and P. G. Wodehouse, standard hit-makers, and I rather imagine that Howard Lindsay and Russel Crouse have aided considerably in making a standard hit of "Anything Goes." Whoever made it, it is made.

The New Yorker, December 8, 1934

STATEMENT

I F IT isn't a feast, it's a famine. I guess that's telling 'em—hey, fat lady? Last week too many plays to crowd into one article, this week not enough to bring us to the bottom of the page without jumping. "Slightly Delirious" was the only opening, and all that has to be said about that can be said in one word. That still leaves quite a lot of words.

Of course, the natural question is: "Why have a Drama page this week at all?" There is no good answer to this. But since there is space at my disposal, I would like to use some of it to clarify the attitude of this department on the current heckling of dramatic critics, which seems to be shaking Society to its very foundations. Already it has reached Fiftieth Street on the north and Forty-first Street on the south. If the wind changes, the whole town may go.

This department is run solely as a superficial guide to readers—if anything. Certain readers who know its departmental likes and dislikes may be able to gather, from a close study of the page, whether or not they might like the show under discussion. As often as not the decision might be: "If he likes it, I'm not going to waste my money on it." The idea is, at any rate, to indicate the possible money value of the new theatrical offerings to each reader personally.

It is not even a news page, for, if you have ever noticed, there is never any possible indication of what the plot is. For that, as they say on the radio, you must "see your daily papers." All that you will get here is the strictly personal reactions of whoever happens to be writing the page. It has nothing to do with the Drama, as such.

So when we are assailed with the charge of jeopardizing the investments of producers or ruining the theatrical business, we are something less than devastated, because the only investment that we have in mind is the investment of three-thirty, or four-forty, on the part of our clients, and with that only slightly.

The theatrical business can be ruined just as effectively by a lot of people losing three-thirty apiece as by a producer losing twenty-five thousand.

The only vestige of conscientiousness that goes into these reviews is that if we leave a show early, we make a note of the fact for our readers' information, and if we doze off, we also indicate it as part of the record of our reactions to that particular production. (One of Mr. Winchell's scouts had us asleep throughout a show at which we stood up back two-thirds of the time, as our seats were occupied by two younger members of the family. It must have been two other Benchleys.) Also, we go back and see a show a second time if there is any doubt in our mind.

Aside from these few slight points of professional honor, there is nothing which goes into the making of this page which is any different from what any ordinary theatregoer would put into it if talking about the theatre at dinner. Any attempt to intimidate us into a more serious attitude will be held as an infringement of the Freedom of the Press.

The New Yorker, January 19, 1935

THE GOVERNMENT TAKES
A HAND

ANEW, and rather exciting, element has crept into the New York theatrical season, just as it was plucking at the coverlet and taking great whiffs of anesthetic spring air. All over town, from Harlem down to Macdougal Street, little groups of hitherto unemployed actors, musicians, and technicians are putting on shows of their own, under the auspices of the federal government, and darned good shows, too, some of them. The five that I have seen have all been definitely worth doing, which is more than you could say for five consecutive shows on Broadway.

The most ambitious, and also the best, of the Federal Theatre offerings so far is "Murder in the Cathedral," the poetic drama by T. S. Eliot, which had already been given an unprofessional performance at Yale. Here, at the Manhattan Theatre, is a production of which any commercial manager would be proud, although probably no commercial manager would undertake it. You can't blame the commercial managers, but you can be glad that the Federal Theatre has come along to give us plays that otherwise we might not see.

Dealing with the murder of Thomas à Becket in the cathedral at Canterbury in 1170, this long dramatic (and it is dramatic) poem of Mr. Eliot's marches at a surprising pace under the direction of Halsted Welles, and, helped considerably by the dignified and persuasive acting of Harry Irvine as the Archbishop and the scenery and costuming of Tom Adrian Cracraft, it turns out to be a valuable contribution to the season and a great credit to the Project.

Not the least important (in fact, to my mind the most important) feature of "Murder in the Cathedral" is its surprising switch toward the end to first-class modern satire, when the four murderers, in the most approved form of Liberty League after-dinner speaking, step to the footlights and justify their violent act in short, impromptu *apologiae*. Sinclair Lewis himself never did a better, or more scathing, job of Fascist kidding, and to one who was unable to follow Mr. Eliot through his "Waste Land" and who has always held him to be without much humor, this veritable masterpiece of parody comes as, shall we say, a thunderbolt, but a thunderbolt calling for loud huzzas.

On the opening night it did get applause, but in one quarter, at least, under a slight misapprehension. A little nest of ardent proletarians, all set to applaud any reference to the Cause, heard one of the speakers say that "under certain circumstances, violence is permissible," and, forgetting that it was *Fascist* violence that was being excused (if they ever understood it), burst into ecstatic handclapping. We must all be very careful to listen to just what cause is being advocated before we applaud a phrase which might apply to several. In fact, these little groups of applauders constitute one of the main nuisances of the Federal Theatre Project.

"Chalk Dust," another of the experimental-theatre productions, is also a play worthy of your attention. You will have to go up to Sixty-third Street to see it, but if you are interested in the problems which confront teachers and educational institutions, or even if you just like to see a good play, it will be worth the trip. Harold Clarke and Maxwell Nurnberg have written of the politics and intrigues which infest a city high school, and they have done it apparently from the heart. The cast is large, as is the cast of every Federal Theatre production, but the cause is good, and God knows the price is low. (Fifty-five cents.) When, in addition to this, the show is good, not much more could be asked.

For some strange reason, the WPA Theatre Project is not allowed to advertise (we must economize *some*where), so the good plays are dependent on word-of-mouth advertising. In the list of attractions in the front of this magazine, you will find the necessary information as to addresses, telephone numbers, and hours of these worthy entertainments.

One of the disadvantages of dealing with WPA productions in a weekly magazine is the short term of their stay. Two or three weeks is usually the limit, although "Chalk Dust," because of its obvious merits, has been granted an indefinite extension, and I hope that "Murder in the Cathedral" will be allowed to continue beyond the date set (March 31st). "Triple-A Plowed Under" may be gone before this notice appears, but if it is not, you will be interested in seeing, in this edition of the "Living Newspaper" at the Biltmore Theatre, how a subject as statistical as wheat production can be put on the stage with considerable excitement and dramatic value.

An unfortunate feature of governmental control of one of the arts seems to be a tendency to factional snarlings and bad-blood spilling. Heads may be in the clouds, but chips are on every shoulder. The lobby of the Biltmore Theatre during the run of "Triple-A Plowed Under" has the tense atmosphere of a high-school foyer on the eve of an inter-sorority debate, and resignations, criminations, and recriminations fly through the air with each production. The letter that I received from Mr. Pierre Loving of the Experimental Theatre, presumably designed to induce me to go and see "Chalk Dust" (which I had already seen), is typical of the jumpy attitude which seems to prevail in government theatrical circles.

"I do not know," writes Mr. Loving, "whether it is a fixed policy with you to avoid Federal Theatre plays . . . You may not like Sixty-third Street nor the idea of an experimental theatre, since you are, as the whole world knows, committed to Broadway and a little tight corner of Hollywood."

Now, Mr. Loving had no reason to be cross with me. I was merely waiting until I had seen enough of the Federal Theatre plays to make up a page like this about them. And, as the tramp said when thrown off the golf course by the chairman of the membership committee, "That's no way to get new members."

The New Yorker, March 28, 1936

"IDIOT'S DELIGHT"

T HE THEATRE GUILD rounds out its season in a veritable blaze of glory, or inferno of cockeyed madness, whichever way you happen to regard a night air raid. For when the final curtain falls on Robert E. Sherwood's "Idiot's Delight," the Next War is on, and this dear, good-natured, irresponsible old world is *at* itself again.

"Idiot's Delight" is a fine combination of rage, despair, and good humor on Mr. Sherwood's part. He cannot believe it possible that grown men will fall for the same old line again so soon, and yet he sees it happening. Having three of the most popular personal souvenirs of the Late War himself (shellshock, gas, and a wound), owing to the imperfect protection afforded his six-feet-six by the kilts of the Canadian Black Watch, Mr. Sherwood doesn't know whether to laugh or cry at the present spectacle, and so he does both, and with splendid effect.

When he laughs, he is at his best and his bitterest. It is impossible to be serious in an argument with people who want war. They know all the answers, or, rather, *the* Answer, which is War. The head of the munitions trust in "Idiot's Delight" didn't mind it a bit when Mr. Sherwood got serious at him, but he was a little confused at the gay tactics of the travelling hoofer. The only way to get around the munitions group is to confuse them until they find themselves in the front-line trenches. This, I admit, will take quite a bit of confusing.

In case this all sounds as if Mr. Sherwood had written a treatise, let it be stated that the scene is a small hotel in what used to be the Austrian Alps (now Italian by that magic which lay in the Versailles Treaty), and that the hero is a road-company Harry Richman, who is stuck there at the outbreak of hostilities with his little flock of cuties who constitute what is vaguely known as "the act." This is Mr. Lunt, and it is Mr. Lunt at his best. It is also Mr. Sherwood at his best. And all that Harry

175

Van, the hoofer, ever asks about the War is "Why?," which, after all, is all that there is to ask.

The heroine is a mysterious blonde Russian, who is travelling as a sideline with the munitions king, and who later turns out to be an Armenian-born trouper who once had made the Governor Bryan Hotel in Omaha, Nebraska, a hallowed spot in the memory of the hoofer. This is Miss Fontanne, and one can easily see what the hoofer means. I'll bet the people at the Governor Bryan remember her, too.

Then there is a vital little Communist, played with great fire and distinction by Richard Whorf, who, although a citizen of the world "with no nationality," turns violently patriotic when the crisis comes and he hears that his native Paris has been bombed by Italian fliers. (The Italian fliers take care of him.) In his one impassioned cry of "Vive la France!" Mr. Sherwood sums up his sad case on the futility of opposition to the mighty forces of insanity.

Other guest rats trapped in the hotel include Sydney Greenstreet as a German scientist who gives up trying to save people from cancer when they insist on being killed by each other, Bretaigne Windust and Jean Macintyre as a pathetic little bridal couple who came only for the winter sports, and Francis Compton as the munitions king, who was hardly surprised at the turn of events. Edward Raquello, in the rôle of the Italian captain, handles the rebuttal with dignity and fairness.

"Idiot's Delight" is a fine play, slightly diffused, perhaps, in its twin allegiance to good entertainment and its lesson, but no more diffused than the elements which go into the world with which it deals. It is one of the few plays which everyone *should* see and which, at the same time, are good shows.

In the matter of high-pressure applause, noted during some of the WPA entertainments and other gatherings of our more determined proletarians, it might be observed that, in its own high-class way, and without giving the slightest offence except a possible pain in the neck, your typical Theatre Guild audience can oversell its enthusiasm about as thoroughly as any group in town.

Guild audiences, naturally, have their little jokes among themselves and their favorites on the stage, although since Helen Westley went to Hollywood they have had a hard time finding someone at whom to laugh regardless. But when Mr. Lunt went into his dance routine in the second act of "Idiot's Delight," it was considered one of the most delectable bits of absurdity in a decade and a spectacle calling for extra-special laughter to the point of polite hysteria.

There is no question that Mr. Lunt does his dance steps amusingly (although, in the light of later passages in the play, they could be considered more than a little sad), but it was not *how* he was doing them that delighted the Guilders so much as it was the utterly screaming idea of Alfred Lunt's doing dance steps. It was as if Professor Copeland had appeared in a Hasty Pudding Club show dressed as a girl.

Now, Mr. Lunt happens to be not only one of the best actors, but easily the most versatile, that we have in this country. He has played every type of rôle, from Clarence to the beast-boy in "Point Valaine," and played them well. There is nothing at all incongruous in his embellishing his rôle of hoofer by doing a little hoofing. It all depends on whether you look at "Idiot's Delight" as the serious play that it is, and Mr. Lunt as the fine actor that he is, or consider the whole thing a Guild Prom Week entertainment. To an outsider, it is not funny to see Mr. Lunt dancing. At any rate, not as funny as all that. I realize that probably Mr. Lunt doesn't mind (although he might very well get sick of it later in the run), and certainly there is no virtue in complaining of audience-enthusiasm in any form; so I guess I'd better shut up.

The New Yorker, April 4, 1936

BIG NAMES

ONFRONTED with both Hamlet and Napoleon in one week, a reviewer must put aside any sly inclination he may have had toward giggling and small talk, and put on his best front, which, God knows, is none too impressive. I don't know what a reviewer can say about either Hamlet or Napoleon, except that they both looked very natural, and that Mr. John Gielgud, in "Hamlet," and Mr. Maurice Evans, in "St. Helena," were excellent in their respective portrayals. However, certain other formalities have to be gone through with.

John Gielgud's Hamlet comes to us from London, where it has had an enormous success. This seems only logical, for it is a Hamlet that you will remember—intelligent, sensitive, and at times inspired to the point of lifting your orchestra chair a few inches off the floor with you in it. It is in its sensitive intelligence, I think, that it excels.

As so often happens, a highly sensitive intelligence sometimes swings around into a neurosis, and there were times when I felt that Mr. Gielgud was letting himself go at the expense of the lines he was reading, but these moments were few and far between. And to complain of Hamlet's being neurotic is, I suppose, like complaining of Ophelia's being mad or of Polonius's being verbose. Hamlet's nerves could not have been what you would call "in the pink." I will take gladly the few jumpy moments that Mr. Gielgud gave me and discount them for the many more moments of genuine excitement.

In case my vote is needed, however, to settle a tie between John Barrymore and John Gielgud, I must admit that for my money (a pass) Mr. Barrymore's Hamlet was more to my liking. There was a humor there, a mad *arrière-pensée*, which happened to fit in with my own personal feeling about Hamlet, for which I hold no brief other than that it *is* personal. Mr. Gielgud smiles, it is true, and smiles at the right times, but it is a sad smile, a smile of infinite sweetness, and bodes no ill to anyone. Mr. Barrymore's smile was the smile of an actor who hates actors, and who know that he is going to kill two or three before the play is over. I am not an actor-killer, but I like my Hamlets to dislike actors, if you know what I mean, and I think you don't.

Aside from my practically unbounded admiration for Mr. Gielgud, I was frankly disappointed in Mr. McClintic's production. This is hard to explain when I have to say that I thought that Judith Anderson was the best Queen I ever saw, that Lillian Gish, in the unfortunate mad scene, was superb, and that Arthur Byron, as Polonius, was as good as you would have a right to expect Arthur Byron to be, which is the best there is.

There was a feeling, however, in my own mind that things were not going well in Denmark. I was afraid for the success of the whole thing, and I was frankly glad when it was over. For the first time, I was definitely not excited by Mr. Mielziner's settings, which in one particular instance reminded me of a dining room in the Bronx, and at other times moved me to nothing more than a mild sigh of satisfaction that things had progressed that far.

In other, and less cagy, words, I think that Mr. Gielgud has to carry his Hamlet on his back, and I think that he is quite capable of doing it.

We now come to Maurice Evans as Napoleon in "St. Helena." I see no reason this should not go down as a fine performance. It made me sorry for Napoleon, and, although Napoleon does not know this, that is quite an achievement. Mr. Evans, who has been known to us here in the wilds in such varied assignments as Romeo and the Dauphin, manages, through some form of necromancy, to *be* Napoleon in this instance, and, if you are anybody at all, makes you feel, by the time of the final curtain, ready to organize a relief expedition to get him out of what must have been the most horrible boredom that a man was ever subjected to, even though he deserved it.

This boredom, in its telling, necessarily involves quite a bit of inaction, but to my mind R. C. Sherriff and Jeanne De Casalis have handled it beautifully and to fine effect. Mr. Sherriff, in his books "The Fortnight in September" and "Green Gates," has proven himself a master of dramatization of inaction, and I am definitely his slave, in case he wants to have me. In "St. Helena," he and Miss De Casalis have shown that inaction can be as tragic as shooting or love, and for this I think that we should all be very grateful to them, inasmuch as they have made a fine play out of it.

The New Yorker, October 17, 1936

PRO FLESH AND BLOOD

STAGE productions involving rocky crags and storms at sea may look pretty sleazy in comparison with movies of their type, and now and then a drawing-room scene in the theatre seems strangely old-fashioned and unreal after some of the expert trickeries of the Silver Screen.

But, boy, when you sit in a theatre and see a stage full of real girls, in real colors, performing chorus numbers in real flesh and blood, and can sit back in your seat (or forward) and take it in all at once with your own eyes, without having to be panned from left to right on camera, then you realize that all the movie millions in the world can't create a spectacle even to approximate it for all-round satisfaction of the senses.

In the first place, no matter how gorgeous the settings and costumes may be for a Hollywood extravaganza when they are being photographed, and no matter how intricate the dance routines may be at the hands of the country's best directors and the feet of the country's best dancers, in the movie theatre they all boil down to a screen the size of an air-mail stamp, where you either get a black-and-white long shot in which you couldn't recognize your own mother, even if you knew her place in the chorus, or a series of rotating closeups showing two-thirds of a body in some sort of individual action, or another series of medium shots, giving you an inkling of what two or three of the people are doing and thinking at that particular moment. That's no way to look at a chorus in action.

Of course, when color photography becomes common, the drab slate-gray note will be relieved and the magnificent colors in which movie musicals are actually made will not be wasted, as they are now, but even then, how are you going to look along a whole line of girls, with one *coup d'oeil*, without having to wait for the whim of the cameraman? How are you going to pick out the one you like the best, and look at her exclusively if you happen to want to? How are you, in other words, going to enjoy a musical show to your heart's content? The movies have taken all Romance out of musicals.

These possibly lecherous remarks have been brought on by the satisfaction of watching the chorus in "Red, Hot and Blue!," one of the too-few real musical shows on Broadway right now. The girls are pretty and have style. Constance Ripley has designed some lovely costumes, and we see them in the colors in which they were designed, not Eastman gray. George Hale has arranged some excellent dances, and we see them being danced all at once and in the same theatre with us, not on a mirrored floor half a mile away. Donald Oenslager's settings are bright and cheerful, and the whole thing makes you feel very warm and gay, and glad that Mr. Vinton Freedley still believes that there should be some excitement about watching a musical comedy.

In the matter of stars, we have Jimmy Durante, Ethel Merman, and Bob Hope. I shall have to control myself in speaking of Mr. Durante, as I sometimes seem prone to overdo my enthusiasm for him and his charms. All that I will say is that I have never seen him better, and let it go at that. Miss Merman is her usual dynamic self, and I have an idea that one or two of Mr. Cole Porter's songs benefit greatly by her powers of projection, although, on a second visit to the show, I was convinced that Mr. Porter's score is much better than I thought it the first time. Certainly "It's De-Lovely," "A Little Skipper from Heaven Above," and "Hymn to Hymen" are first grade, and if he wanted to make "Down in the Depths, on the 90th Floor" another version of "Night and Day," he had a perfect right to. His lyrics are, as usual, in a class by themselves.

In the matter of the book of Messrs. Lindsay and Crouse, I feel that they rather underestimated their own taste when they settled on the mark of a hot waffle iron on a young lady's *derrière* as their theme and then proceeded to pun their way ahead in the same vein, but as far as I am concerned, Mr. Hope can carry quite a lot of corny dialogue without giving offence (Heaven knows he has had to in the past) and he helps Miss Polly Walters in her even more difficult assignment. The Hartmans, as incidental comedy of their own devising, are also an addition.

Of course, it is probably unfair to say that the book is under par and then say that Mr. Durante has never been funnier, for the authors presumably were in the same building when his material was being devised. If he is at his best, and Miss Merman sings Mr. Porter's music, and the chorus is beautiful to look at, what is there really to cavil at?

181

And to get back to our thesis, there is a new musical comedy in town which makes any million-dollar Hollywod production look like just what it is—a moving picture on a screen.

The New Yorker, November 7, 1936

"TONIGHT AT 8:30"

THAT there is a Noel Coward legend in New York, even a Noel Coward fixation, is obvious to anyone who can tie a white tie and get about. And yet, remarkable among cases of mass hypnosis of this type, there is a basis of solid reason to the thing. Mr. Coward may dazzle us by the multiplicity of his accomplishments, some of which, like his singing voice, veer slightly leeward, but, when all is said and done, he furnishes just about as practical and honest an evening's entertainment as you could find in the theatre.

Mr. Coward is a necromancer, but that doesn't interfere with his show's being good entertainment. Out of several very ordinary silk hats, some of them even seedy, he pulls live rabbits which not only are cute but can imitate other animals, such as swans, jaguars, doves, and dik-diks. They may still be rabbits, and they may be out of old hats, but I, personally, would just as soon have them as the real thing, so long as Mr. Coward cracks the whip. (I don't suppose that one cracks a whip at rabbits, except in Krafft-Ebing, but that's none of *my* business.)

Out of the nine one-act plays which constitute the Coward Ring (three an evening for three evenings), there are not more than two or three that can actually be said to violate tradition in their essentials. In the first group, we have no plot at all, about a hostess who is amiably vague concerning the identity of her guests ("Hands Across the Sea"), a psychiatrist who finds himself confronted with an emotional crisis of his own ("The Astonished Heart"), and two music-hall comics whose feud with the orchestra leader results in an out-and-out pratt fall ("Red Peppers").

In the second group, Mr. Coward shows us that a romance begun on the dance floor can grow pretty seedy along about six a.m. when the music has stopped ("We Were Dancing"), that a henpecked husband can turn like a worm and rend his wife and mother-in-law when pushed too far ("Fumed Oak"), and, in "Shadow Play," that a marriage which seems headed for the rocks may be salvaged by a trip Down Memory Lane.

In Group Three we are treated to the burglar *ex machina* who saves the day by playing straight man ("Ways and Means"), a futile adultery between respectable married people which, like Cyrano, is cheated even out of its death ("Still Life"), and a family group after a funeral who find that their grief is easily assuaged by a little Madeira and a peek at the will ("Family Album").

Surely, with one or two exceptions, there is no topic here to make you exclaim, "The man is bewitched with originality!" And yet, by the time Mr. Coward has got them out of the hat, they have taken on fresh forms, and, as in the case of "Fumed Oak," you forget that you are watching the old gag of the Turning Worm and the Mother-in-Law in its most elementary state. Through the author's unfailing use of mere words for comedy purposes, "Hands Across the Sea," "We Were Dancing," "Ways and Means" and "Family Album" are lifted high out of the class of anecdotes and become delicious morsels of theatre. "The Astonished Heart," "Shadow Play," and "Still Life," of the more serious plays, all have, as saving graces, Mr. Coward's observation of people and his gift for making a phrase do the work of the old-fashioned dagger. The ending to "Still Life," in which two helpless people have their last minutes stolen from them, is a marvellous example of the tragedy of the trivial.

Working hand in glove with Mr. Coward in the acting and singing ends is Miss Gertrude Lawrence, who has never looked lovelier or acted better. She is a constant delight, as the saying goes. The rest of the cast is appropriately excellent, with Miss Joyce Carey lending invaluable aid in the pinches and Anthony Pelissier, Alan Webb, and others combining to make a smooth-running team.

In the introduction to the book of collected playlets in "Tonight at 8:30," Mr. Coward says:

"The primary object of the scheme is to provide a full and varied evening's entertainment for theatregoers."

No matter which bill you choose, this is what you are pretty sure to get.

The New Yorker, December 5, 1936

DIVIDED OPINION

LET'S begin with the one I am sure about. "You Can't Take It With You" is a very funny show. It is so funny that even when you are not laughing, you get a glow, for it is not only funny but nice.

Moss Hart and George S. Kaufman have put aside the snake whip and have gone in for just plain, old-fashioned humor, at which they seem to excel. The story of a madcap family is not new, neither is the "Trelawney of the Wells" account of young love in conflict with patrician parents, but nothing really matters in "You Can't Take It With You" so long as Grandpa Vanderhof practices his dart-throwing and snake breeding and gets up to Columbia Commencement once a year. (That's the kind of play it is—dart-throwing, snake-breeding, and Columbia Commencement.)

There are times when one wishes that Messrs. Hart and Kaufman had really tried to write a play, which they very easily could have done, as they have done it before. Along about the middle of the second act, the situation begins to cry out for a play instead of a parlor game. But this is really picayune fault-finding, for nobody in the audience really wants a play when he can get the brand of laughs that "You Can't Take It With You" is full of.

I suppose that there are people who won't think that "You Can't Take It With You" is so awfully funny, for there are people who don't see anything funny in crazy families with printing presses and xylophones in the living room and contentment in their hearts. With such critics I have no traffic. The people that I like are the people who like "You Can't Take It With You."

I also like people who like the cast that Sam Harris has assembled for this improbable harlequinade. Henry Travers, after years of hovering around on the edges of an ideal rôle, has at last found one in Grandpa Vanderhof. There are spots of greatness in Mr. Travers' portrayal of the old gentleman who decided to stop work thirty-five years ago because it was interfering with his leisure, and who hadn't paid an income tax for twenty-two years because he didn't believe in it. There are also many fine moments in the life of Josephine Hull, as the mother who took to writing plays because a typewriter had been left at the house by mistake (how many plays are written that way!), but who had just as soon paint or do anything. Paula Trueman is the daughter who ballets her way through life, but who, according to George Tobias, her teacher, "stinks." Frank Conlan, as Mr. DePinna, the iceman, who came to the house eight years ago and liked it so much that he lived there ever since, helping Frank Wilcox, as the father, make illicit fireworks in the cellar, is also an integral part of the great, lovable assemblage, as are the two colored assistants, Ruth Attaway and dear Oscar Polk. And George Heller, the unfortunate young man whose penchant for xylophone-playing and printing cluttered up the living room so, cannot be forgotten in a summary of the pleasures of "You Can't Take it With You." Neither can Mr. Kaufman's direction.

The fact that one has to mention everybody in the play and say what he does is a good indication of what "You Can't Take It With You" is like. It isn't a good play, but it is just about the best evening's entertainment in town, and you are very pleased with yourself for liking it, which is something.

I don't know what got into me that I didn't like "Brother Rat." Everybody else did. And when I say "everybody else," I mean all the reviewers and practically everybody in the audience. I am going to see it again and find out what I could have been thinking of.

In the first place, I was thinking that Virginia Military Institute is a prep school, which apparently it isn't, and it threw me into an evil humor to see the rôles of prep-school boys being played by obviously grown men. Right there I got off on the wrong foot.

Then, and on the same foot, the whole thing struck me as being very Brown-of-Harvard-and-Stover-at-Yale, and, on the whole, a little embarrassing. This mood was not helped by the V.M.I. friends in the audience, who applauded every reference to the little secrets of life at V.M.I. and gave an air of Hasty Pudding to the evening which grew more and more oppressive as the night wore on. One felt that the cast were going to show up in makeup at the buffet supper at Prexy's after the performance. And considering that one or two of the "boys" were on the gangster side of twenty-five, this prospect was slightly appalling.

However, I must have been in the wrong, for my colleagues to a man agreed that here was a pleasant comedy worthy of everybody's attention. In fact, I haven't spoken to anybody who has seen it who didn't like it. So let's put it down to something I ate, and I'll take another crack at it soon. I hate to be as wrong as that.

The New Yorker, December 26, 1936

"BABES IN ARMS"

S EVERAL years ago, when all the world (except Justices McReynolds, Van Devanter, Sutherland, and Butler, and sometimes Roberts and Y) was young, the songwriting team of Rodgers and Hart emerged as forces in the international scene, surrounded by an appealingly noisy gang of youngsters of their own age, in what has since come to be lovingly referred to as "The Garrick Gaieties." (It was referred to as "The Garrick Gaieties" then, too, but not with nostalgia in the voice.)

Messrs. Rodgers and Hart must have had a very soft spot in their hearts for the old "Garrick Gaieties," for they have, all by themselves, reverted to the middle twenties and written a book and score for "Babes in Arms" which call for a horde of young talent and a surge of youthful spirit unheard of since the days when Betty Starbuck, Libby Holman, Romney Brent, Sterling Holloway, and what seemed like thousands of other kids were all bouncing around the stage to the immortal tunes of "Mountain Greenery" and "Manhattan." They have brought a bucketful of water back from the old spring, and it certainly tastes good after that old Scotch and soda.

I had no idea that there were so many young people still alive as appear from every nook and cranny of "Babes in Arms." They are all over the place, singing, dancing, cracking wise (but not too wise, mind you), and, what is even more remarkable, without offence. They are all experts in their lines, and they have the good manners of experts. This is no stage children's matinée, calling for machine-gun fire from the audience. It is a swell show, acted by young people who know their business. There's no harm in that, is there?

Dwight Deere Wiman took quite a sporting chance when he elected to put on a musical comedy without big names (except those of Rodgers and Hart) and he has gone through with it valiantly, and, as it turns out, with great success. Of course,

188

Mitzi Green is a name, in a way, but not a name that has become associated with musical comedy in the minds of the "wise money." Unless I miss my guess, however, it has already become so associated, and here it is only Wednesday. Miss Green (if I may call her Miss Green at the age of sixteen) can put over a song, among other things, with authority and humor, and will probably soon be back in Hollywood, which was her professional cradle.

It is difficult to list the young stars who contribute to the general effect of effervescence, but there are Ray Heatherton, who sings with the voice that radio listeners know; Duke McHale, who dances, especially effectively in a fantastic ballet arranged by Balanchine, which is one of the highlights of the show; Wynn Murray, a young lady of considerable proportions and comedy value in the lyric passages; Rolly Pickert; the McDonalds, sister and brother; and, as a continual delight, both in eye-rolling and shoe-tapping, the dark *frères* Nicholas, who could carry a show by themselves. There are others, and still others, who seem to come out of nowhere, but who are definitely headed for somewhere, and if you think these names don't mean very much now, all right for *you*.

Coming back to Rodgers and Hart, as people are likely to be doing during the summer months, they have turned out one of their nicest scores. "Babes in Arms," which starts the show off with what is technically known as "a bang," has a crusading, evangelical quality about its rising surge which might well be used for a more sturdy Youth Movement than organizing a vaudeville show in a barn, which is the plot of the play. (Incidentally, the plot gets in the way quite a bit, especially toward the end, when a whole new show seems to be in the process of construction, with a new set of characters and almost a new management. I was frankly at sea during the last fifteen minutes, and thought that I had got back into the wrong theatre.) There are other excellent numbers, too numerous to mention, because, until you have seen the show, you won't give a damn. However, you'll see the show, I'm sure.

The New Yorker, April 24, 1937

189

SHAKESPEARE AGAIN

I T TURNS out that there are two ways of doing Shakespeare: the old way and the good way. The good way, now on view at the Mercury Theatre, where "Julius Caesar" is being played, comes as something of a surprise to those of us who had grown rather benign between our cat naps at the old rataplan Shakespeare. In fact, it woke us up.

Orson Welles and his Mercury Theatre Group (I take it for granted that it is a group) have put on "Julius Caesar" in modern Fascist trappings, without scenery but with an enormous amount of intelligence. It is a strange experience to be sitting and watching Shakespeare in the raw and to see for yourself just *why* it is good. Mr. Welles himself as Brutus, Mr. Coulouris as Antony, and all the rest of the mob who used to be tripping over their togas in the old days give a reality to the thing which I think might fool the Bard himself. We have had Shakespeare in modern dress before, but, I think, never so vitally or successfully. I don't want to see "All's Well That Ends Well" done in the same style (in fact, I don't want to see "All's Well That Ends Well"), but if "Julius Caesar was an experiment, then Mr. Welles may go right ahead from now on. He has got something there.

As an example of "the old way" of doing Shakespeare, we have the Laurence Rivers production of "Antony and Cleopatra" recently at the Mansfield (if any method involving the services of Miss Tallulah Bankhead may be called "the old way"), and compared with the Orson Welles "Julius Caesar," it was pretty much fustian. Trumpets blew and drums rolled between the scenes in the approved Shakespearian manner of indicating offstage hell-to-pay, and male characters laughed much too heartily in chorus at the parting of each curtain to show a camaraderie and high spirits unwarranted by the text, but we still were watching Shakespeare as it was done in the old Thomas F. Shea days, and in some instances almost identical performances. It was an expensive production and striking to look at, but Mr. Welles' is inexpensive and nothing to look at, so the secret of their difference cannot lie in that quarter.

Since we know so little about Cleopatra (except you know what), I see no reason for complaining that Miss Bankhead doesn't resemble her in looks or manner. For all that we know, Miss Bankhead *was* Cleopatra in an earlier incarnation, which would be a good joke on the critics if it turned out to be so. My chief complaint over Miss Bankhead's performance would be that she had a tendency to wax unintelligible in the clinches, a fault shared by several of her team-mates, all of which is too bad, considering the hard work that Shakespeare must have put in on his wording. Conway Tearle's Antony was in the best Roman tradition, but John Emery's Caesar combined tradition with a moderation which made it easier to take. Thomas Chalmers, in an emasculated version of Enobarbus' meaty rôle, did all that could be done.

After the performance of "Antony and Cleopatra" on Wednesday evening, I was pretty sure that I had taken my 1937-38 course in Shakespeare (usually a very short course, at the pleasure of the pupil in this case). After "Julius Caesar" later in the week, I think I'll stick.

The New Yorker, November 20, 1937

* * *

ONCE again Mr. Orson Welles has demonstrated his skill in staging an old play like a new one. Thomas Dekker's "The Shoemaker's Holiday" could be (and has been, in my college days) done with nothing to recommend it but its high spirits. The production at the Mercury is, I should say, just about perfect for an Elizabethan comedy. The setting is startlingly effective in its simplicity and lighting, and the cast, which includes Whitford Kane, Vincent Price, Edith Barret, Marian Warring-Manley, Hiram Sherman, who leads all the rest in clowning, and others of the Mercury group, is more than good enough for such a romp. "The Shoemaker's Holiday" will share the stage at the Mercury with "Caesar" until February, and you will have to look in the papers to see which is which on any particular night, but you can't lose, whichever one you hit.

The New Yorker, January 8, 1938

TWO AT ONCE

DEATH stalked two stages on two successive nights last week, the Longacre's in a joyous, delectable fantasy by Paul Osborn called "On Borrowed Time" and the Henry Miller's in a beautifully written but more conventionally conceived tone poem by Thornton Wilder called "Our Town." Both plays added immeasurably to the season's excitement.

Jed Harris will probably kill me for calling "Our Town" conventional, for he has gone to a great deal of pains to make it unconventional, almost too great pains at times. He has produced it on a bare stage (which is almost getting to be old-hat by now) and he has eschewed such petty aids to illusion as props. He even refused to pass out programs until the last act, with the result that I got no program. Frank Craven, in the manner of the old Property Man in "The Yellow Jacket," moves what chairs and tables there are and draws the curtains, commenting during the action from the corner of the proscenium and telling us when to go home. In the minds of all concerned it was evidently considered a "departure," if not an "experiment."

But the fact remains that if it were not for Mr. Wilder's inspired words, "Our Town" would be just another of those series of episodes in small-town life of the early nineteen-hundreds dealing with the lives, loves, and deaths of the average American of that day. It happens to be a poignant and affecting record, but playing it half in speech and half in dumb show, half with real chairs and half with imaginary lawn-mowers and string beans, adds nothing to its value. To me, as a matter of fact, it was an almost irritating affectation. The use of pantomime in such detailed routines as flapjack-making is a silly procedure at best, suited more for charades and other guessing games, and a serious script has a hard time standing up under the disadvantage of having the audience trying to guess what in hell the characters are supposed to be doing with their hands. That several of Mr. Wilder's scenes emerge refulgent from all this sign language and wigwagging is a great tribute to his powers as a writer and dramatist. It is all very charming when the Chinese do it, but Mr. Wilder did not write a charming play and we are not Chinese.

That a great many people were not as bothered as I was by all this *Ersatz* is attested by the fact that I have found few who were not honestly affected by "Our Town." I was affected, too, some of the time by the slightly unfair use of "Blest Be the Tie That Binds" and other nostalgic hymns in the clinches (a ruse for which I am a sucker) and some of the time by the honest and sympathetic performances of the actors, especially Mr. Craven's (his whole soul was in it, you could feel that) and those of his son John and Miss Martha Scott, the latter, I imagine, the personification of the girl that every man fell in love with at least once when he was young. The scene in the graveyard on the hill, with the dead chatting about the weather bolt upright in their chairs and the living hiding their lack of understanding under wet umbrellas, is a haunting and genuinely imaginative piece of staging. Incidentally, there is no pantomime here.

There is no doubt that any season could count itself proud to bring forth "Our Town." For my part, I wish that I could have given my whole attention to it.

There is no trouble in giving your whole attention to "On Borrowed Time." Here is a play which might have been just a touch on the whimsical side, with its personification of Death as a "Mr. Brink" in a top coat who gets stuck up in a tree and can't come down until an old gentleman tells him to. In fact, it sounds pretty cute just to tell about. But, take it from me, it is nothing of the sort. It is a heart-warming, delightful play that Mr. Osborn has written and it is played in a heart-warming, delightful manner by the actors Dwight Wiman has done us the favor of assembling.

The story really is that of the love of a little boy for his "Gramps" and of "Gramps" for the little boy, and not even Death can do anything about it. Even Death, or Mr. Brink, sees their point and turns out to be quite a decent chap after all. As Gramps, Dudley Digges gives one of the best performances of his career, making swearing, mild lechery, and even dying all major virtues. The little boy has to be so small that alternates must be used in the part. It was played by Peter Holden the night I saw it, and he is unbelievable. That is the only word for it—unbelievable. There are two courses that you have a choice of while he is onstage, laughing or crying, so you do both. Frank Conroy, as Mr. Brink, also seems to be the ideal selection for a rôle that must have been very difficult to cast, and Dorothy Stickney, Jean Adair, and the rest of the players all seem cognizant of the fact that they are integral parts in an event which is going to give joy to a great many people. Incidentally, the play is made from a novel by Lawrence Edward Watkin which I have not read but which I am rushing to this minute.

At any rate, the sum of these two plays dealing with Death in two distinct manifestations, one gay and the other sombre, leads to the comforting thought expressed by Mr. Housman when he wrote, "Life, to be sure, is nothing much to lose."

The New Yorker, February 12, 1938

"THE SEA GULL"

I T IS A little late to come dashing up with laudatory comment or disparaging cracks about "The Sea Gull." The thing has more or less been threshed out, and the verdict, I should say, has been favorable. It may not be the most incisive play of Chekhov's, but any incision at all by Chekhov is a good clean cut.

All that remains, therefore, is to give a thought to the Theatre Guild production and then go home. Here again we are dealing in almost foregone conclusions, for the Guild has rushed its big guns into this final stand of the season and the Lunts couldn't very well fail to make "The Sea Gull" interesting. Arkadina and Trigorin are their dish, and they get the full flavor from it, both for the audience and for themselves.

Since the play is little more than a study of how two veterans in the arts can mess up the lives of two beginners, all that we have to do is sit back and watch them do it, and Miss Fontanne and Mr. Lunt do a lovely job of messing-up. A fresh translation by Stark Young adds immeasurably to the pace and ease of the action, and Robert Edmond Jones' settings combine reality with a vague biliousness which gives you the feeling that even though things look all right, they are really far from it.

As the two unhappy novices, Richard Whorf and a newcomer named Uta Hagen are excellent contrasts to the callous facility of the Lunts. We all know Mr. Whorf's versatility, which overcomes a startling resemblance to Eddie Cantor to make us really believe in his mental agony (not that Eddie Cantor doesn't give off mental agony, too, but not Chekhovian), and I venture to say that Miss Hagen is a definite find. Her eager listening to Trigorin's words as he holds forth for her benefit marks her as an actress who needs no lines for herself, but when she does have them, she makes them sing. Margaret Webster also comes off with considerable triumph as Masha, especially in the drinking scene, and Sydney Greenstreet, from his chair, gives full value to some of the meatier lines of the play.

Even though "The Sea Gull" may not prove much as a social document, the present production does prove that the Guild can still put on a fine play in fitting fashion.

The Guild's policy of seating no late-comers until the end of the first scene reached its logical conclusion at the opening of "The Sea Gull." All those who came in after the curtain had gone up stood in the back until the end of the first act, Chekhov having neglected to divide his first act into scenes.

On this question, as on all others, this department takes a firm stand. Both sides are right and both sides are wrong. If you have managed to get in on time and have any idea of doing the right thing by the play, then late-comers should not only be kept standing at the back but should be slightly tortured with hot irons while they stand. If, on the other hand, you happen to be three minutes late, owing to your hostess, or a waiter, or a premonitory wave of nausea, you have a well-justified sense of being put-upon by an over-snooty organization of intellectuals when you are kept standing during a whole act of Chekhov.

The question is not whether the Guild is right, for it undoubtedly is. But is it wise? Which is worse for the play—twenty-five people straggling in after the curtain has gone up, or twenty-five people standing up at the back snarling at the Guild throughout the first act. Here again this department comes out squarely on the issue. I don't know. (I must admit that an offer was made, in view of my age and official standing, to seat me when I came in three minutes late, but I refused it with what I meant to be caustic graciousness, feeling that if Herbert Bayard Swope were to be kept standing, I could stand too.)

The New Yorker, April 9, 1938

"THE BOYS FROM SYRACUSE"

S INCE "The Boys from Syracuse" seems headed for a triumphal course into the spring months, I might as well lead off with all the good things I found in it, which were plenty. In the first place, it has the best score that Rodgers and Hart have given us for some time; in fact, for a longer time than that. Right there you have reason enough for its success, for a Grade-A Rodgers and Hart score is Grade-A entertainment, regardless of its surroundings. Its surroundings, in this case, happen to be fairly reeking with class, so that end is taken care of very nicely. George Abbott has given it one of those productions which make you sure you are witnessing a hit, even if you don't happen to be.

Then there is Jimmy Savo, who for a sure-fire comic has run into an unconscionable amount of hard luck of late, but who now, much to everybody's joy, can glide his way in circles to his heart's content, leering that completely unconvincing leer and indulging in that pantomime which has few equals today. Teddy Hart manages to do the impossible and act as Savo's double without making you long too much for Savo (Mr. Hart's solo about his Big Brother is something all his own and calls for no comparison with anyone else). Then there are such personable performers as Eddie Albert, Ronald Graham, and the Misses Muriel Angelus and Marcy Wescott, and the beaming singer of the hot B-flat, Wynn Murray (of "Johnny One-Note" fame), all of whom sing Mr. Rodgers' music and Mr. Hart's lyrics to what I think must be better than the Queen's taste. Here, surely, is enough pleasure for one evening.

But once more I must be in a minority in thinking that Shakespeare's "The Comedy of Errors" could not be made into a funny story, even by George Abbott. Mr. Abbott can do wonders, but trying to make the tale of the twin masters and twin slaves into even passable comedy (rollicking, yes—but not passable) was, from my seat, too tough an assignment. Without Mr. Savo's personality, which

197

he had before the show, and Frère Hart's shadowing, my own personal laughter would have been confined to the lyrics, and there seemed to be quite a few long stretches between song numbers.

I also submit a minority report that there was too much ballet, that the curtain to the first act about letting Acidophilus (or whatever his name was) in was nerve-racking, and that a dance number which tried to combine tap and ballroom dancing was simply terrible.

I now rejoin the majority (if they will have me) and go on record as recommending "The Boys from Syracuse," if only for the score and Jimmy Savo.

The New Yorker, December 3, 1938

QUESTIONS WITHOUT ANSWERS

ALMOST as if it were the result of a pre-season junta of playwrights at which the slogan "Sell America!" had been adopted, the theatre this year has rung with exhortations for us all to hold dear our national heritage and be Americans.

Aside from the fact that it would be difficult *not* to be an American if you are one already, and overlooking a slight feeling of resentment at being told by any other Americans to Buck Up, the general effect of this campaign must be fairly vague, as the playwrights themselves have been fairly vague in their outlines of what constitutes Americanism. Robert E. Sherwood seems to have been the most practical one of his craft. He simply gave us Abraham Lincoln and let us look at him.

The question here is not how skillfully the playwrights have done their work, but just whom is it aimed at. Who are these renegade fellow-Americans who need arousing, and, once they are aroused, what are they going to do about it? How are we dilatory patriots to know when we have reached that fine pitch of American-ism which indicates that we have made the grade and need have no more plays reminding us of our heritage?

Among the problems which it would seem that an American might well have to face, along with the implied ones of Nazi intrusion and other alien influences, is what to do with those Americans who have no jobs. It is presumably not their fault that they have no jobs. It may be the System, it may be the American Tradition, which sent us off on a great Big War and brought us back into a great Big Mess (see "The American Way"), or it may be just tough luck. Whatever the reason, not many people like to be without jobs, especially actors, for acting is their dish.

And so, when an organization like the Federal Theatre, which has, much to everyone's surprise and some folks' confusion, not only justified its foundation but given the American Theatre an impetus at the time when it needed it, is forced to lay off thousands of workers because Congress has suddenly decided to get tough (by one vote), one wonders just what practical Americanism really is and who the dreamers are.

All that is necessary for anyone who knows the Theatre is to look back over the list of Federal Theatre productions to see that it has been no crack-brained scheme, like shooting off hundreds of thousands of dollars' worth of shells at naval maneuvers. "Power," "One-Third of a Nation," "Haiti" (in Harlem), "Murder in the Cathedral," "Macbeth" (in Harlem), "Dr. Faustus," "Androcles and the Lion" (in Harlem), "Pinocchio", and "Horse Eats Hat" all have been definite contributions to the art of our theatre. It may be that the Theatre is not a practical art. If you think so, forget it. The question still remains: "What is to be done with the people who have no jobs?" You can't forget that, if you are an American.

And, to get back into our gay mood again (for Americans are notoriously gay), why is it that a lady singer in a Gilbert and Sullivan production can be flat all over the place and nobody minds, whereas I, if I try to sing in a group, can hit only one flat note before I am thrown out on my face?

The better the music, the more lady singers are allowed to flat. Male singers—no. Just the ladies, and just the *good* singers. Opera singers can flat, and Gilbert and Sullivan singers can flat, but Benchley can't flat. Is that fair?

The New Yorker, February 4, 1939

GOING OVERBOARD FOR
ETHEL MERMAN

T HIS IS a pretty late date for me to be going overboard for Ethel Merman, but I like to take my time in such matters. It also makes it easier to explain, as almost everyone in New York already knows what I mean.

In "Stars in Your Eyes," however, I do think that she shows for the first time that she has a genuine talent as a comedienne in addition to her well-established ability to hold one note and shake her bracelets. As the Hollywood star who brooks no interference in her love plans, and later as a Russian princess with Jimmy Durante (I know that the connection isn't clear, but neither is the plot), she displays such a firm grasp of the art of comic acting that she has it practically by the throat. If I am late in discovering it, all right, I've been a dope. She's got me now.

"Stars in Your Eyes" is Dwight Deere Wiman's latest contribution to his own hit parade, and is J. P. McEvoy's contribution to the parade of Hollywood satires. It is not so much that we were all crazy mad to see another Hollywood satire, but most of us were anxious to see Miss Merman and Jimmy Durante again, and here is a chance to see them both in rare form.

If I have been slow in catching onto Miss Merman's varied talents, I was so early in my adoration of Mr. Durante that often in the past dozen years I have been suspected of nepotism in his case. (There's a word for you, James, and it doesn't mean anything to bring a blush to your cheek.)

There are also several other sterling characters in "Stars in Your Eyes," including Richard Carlson, who brings a bucolic freshness to the rôle of an idealistic young writer of folk movies, and Mildred Natwick, who calls for a sentence all by herself. For several years we have been hailing Miss Natwick for her distinguished portrayals, in the legitimate theatre, of grandmothers, housekeepers, spinsters, and "senior citizens" in general, but this is the first time that we have been able to realize that she is not only a personable young lady but also an expert in the ways of *légère* and unmannered comedy, knowing exactly what is going on and throwing it away, as if all her life she had been roaming around a musical show and could be surprised at nothing. I have for some time been toying with an idea for Miss Natwick to play Ophelia with a quiet, inhibited tenseness in the mad scenes in place of the ga-ga, wind-blown romp to which we are accustomed, and I now turn the suggestion over to some producer in all confidence.

Then, as we have come to expect from Mr. Wiman, there is a ballet dancer, this time the agile Tamara Toumanova, fresh out of the Monte Carlo Ballet Russe and obviously top-notch. For me, a little ballet goes a long way, and there seems to be no such thing as "a little ballet". The young ladies all remind me of Fannie Brice when they drop back onto the flat of the foot after coming down from their toes (they don't remind me *enough* of Fanny Brice, however), but I suppose that the ballet is here to stay after all that publicity by Degas, and I must admit that it has plenty of adherents.

Arthur Schwartz's music and Dorothy Fields' lyrics seem just right for "Stars in Your Eyes," and Miss Merman's number called "I'll Pay the Check" sounds like one of her best, possibly not from a dance-orchestra point of view, but certainly as a piece of adult writing. And, speaking of orchestras, Al Goodman's band has some lovely orchestrations to execute, which help no end.

So let us say that "Stars in Your Eyes" is an all-round good show, a bit on the slow side in getting started, but whipping into superior entertainment as it goes along, and it certainly goes along.

The New Yorker, February 18, 1939

"THE LITTLE FOXES"

MISS LILLIAN HELLMAN evidently knows the box where the fruit-cake is hidden in the dramaturgic pantry, for she fills her plays with good, rich raisins and solid theatrical fare—a little indigestible, possibly, but awfully, awfully good. "The Little Foxes" is a play to put into a small box and tuck under your pillow at night. You may have nightmares, but they will do you good.

Just as in her first play, "The Children's Hour," you realized as the story unfolded that you were sitting in on a real piece of dramatic writing, so in "The Little Foxes" it doesn't take long to find out that here is a tightly woven, well-conceived, and probably very significant contribution to the theatre. The fact that it panders in no way to what the public might possibly want makes it even better. Miss Hellman evidently had this play in her mind and wrote it, and wrote it as well as she could write it, which is tops. The public can take it or leave it, but if they take my advice, they'll take it.

The Hubbards are not a pleasant family. There is almost nothing pleasant about "The Little Foxes." But there is also nothing pleasant about the little foxes in American life, "the little foxes that spoil the vines." They do, however, make up into nice material for a sinister play about sinister people, and this family of old Southern gentlemen and ladies who let nothing stand in their way, especially each other, when it comes to bond-lifting and other banking practices, represent a type of good, solid American whom it would be well to keep an eye on.

Aside from the fact that "The Little Foxes" is a play for a theatre that needs it badly, it also is welcome for giving Miss Tallulah Bankhead a part worthy of her talents. No more frippery for Miss Bankhead and no more co'n pone. She plays the part of the bitchy sister in a family of double-pressure heels with a dignity and a drive that she must have been waiting years to unloose. It is a suitable reward for an actress who has for the most part of her career been condescending to play the rôles assigned to her, not condescending in manner but somewhere in the back of her mind.

Miss Patricia Collinge, too, is here given something to do that must give her great satisfaction as an actress. It certainly gives great satisfaction to those out front. The scenes which are hers are *hers*, and they are also scenes. Miss Hellman writes for the actors (and the audience, by the same token) and in the pitiful, tortured character of Birdie (what a name for—well, just what a name!) she has given Miss Collinge a chance to show what she really can do. Not that we needed to be shown, but it is good to be reminded again.

The rest of the cast, under the direction of Herman Shumlin, do not deserve to be grouped under the heading of "the rest of the cast," but time and space do not permit going overboard. Frank Conroy, as Nemesis in a wheelchair; Carl Benton Reid, Dan Duryea, Charles Dingle, and naturally Lee Baker, all group together as protagonists of Miss Hellman's theme, and Florence Williams manages to come through as the White Hope in what might be called a "perfect cast."

Somewhere in this review there must have crept in the feeling that I though "The Little Foxes" is a good play. It is more than that.

The New Yorker, February 25, 1939

CRITICS' ANNIVERSARIES

L AST WEEK was open week for saying "Nyah-nyah!" at the dramatic critics. "Hellz-a-Poppin," well into its second year on Broadway, offered a new version for the coming year, while "Tobacco Road" celebrated the beginning of its record-breaking seventh year by sending Will Geer in to get his letter as Jeeter Lester. (They have only Maurice Evans and Monty Woolley left under wraps for succeeding Jeeters.) The success of both of these productions is hailed as a bitter pill for the critics, just as "Abie's Irish Rose" was before them.

Although I never notice what my critical colleagues say about plays (except to have a complete file of their reviews at my elbow for consultation as I write my own), I do know that this department can face the present campaign of calumny with wide-eyed innocence, or as wide-eyed as its eyes will allow. Certainly nothing was ever said in this space which was derogatory in any way to either of these two popular favorites. On the contrary.

Mr. Walter Winchell is credited with having been the sole sponsor of "Hellz-a-Poppin" when it burst forth, fighting the good fight against formidable odds during those first grim days of October, 1938. But may I quote how this department, under the sensitive baton of Mr. Gibbs, reacted in the issue of October 1st of that year:

> . . .I had a good time. . .there were very few dull moments, although many strange ones. . . .I think they [the acts] are all lowdown and wonderful. This opinion, however, comes from a man who once considered an afternoon at the Palace the richest cultural experience in life.

Surely the success of "Hellz-a-Poppin" could have come as no surprise to Mr. Gibbs, or to the present guest conductor, who had a swell time at the show when he saw it without portfolio. In the current "new" edition most of the old favorites have been retained and several fresh ones added, notably "The Old Op'ry House," presided over by Charles Withers of old-time vaudeville fame, in which we see Messrs. Olsen and Johnson, with cohorts, in such forceful plays-within-a-play as "The Return of the Cossacks," "Episode at Bunker Hill," and "Public Enemy at the Doorway of Hell," all with spectacular sound effects by Mr. Withers.

The same migratory madness throughout the audience still prevails, however; the Radio Rogues perform their remarkable vocal imitations when they can make themselves heard over the impulsive applause of the dopes in the audience, and the final number, "Surprise Party," proved so surprising that your correspondent found himself with a large and restless hen in his lap, which, as the evening wore on, turned out to be quite a pal.

It must be admitted that the nervous shock of having portions of the auditorium and stray spectators in a constant state of flux is not so great this second time as it was the first, but it serves to keep alive a pleasant apprehension nevertheless and to remind us that "Man is no star, but a quick coal of mortal fire."

To return to the Shame of the Critics, let us consider "Tobacco Road" and see what this department said about it in the issue of December 16, 1933:

> It would be possible to write a burlesque of "Tobacco Road". . .but somehow you don't want to. There is a certain quality about the play. . .which brings one up just short of giggling. It has the strange dishevelled dignity of sounding true. . .one has to go back to Katherine Mansfield's "The Doll's House" for a more devastating example of tragic imperviousness to the bludgeonings of Fate.

Nothing to put up in lights, perhaps, but certainly friendly. The qualities which we discovered in the play may not have been the ones which have kept it running for six years, but Mr. Kirkland, the author, certainly cannot shake his gory locks at us as a potential murderer.

And while we are on the subject, let's settle this "Abie's Irish Rose" thing once and for all. Popular legend had it that I predicted that it would not run a week. With each successive anniversary of the show I was presented with a birthday cake by the management, a candle for every year it had run. I even made a speech at the fifth birthday party, simulating pretty confusion.

As a matter of fact, the only prediction that I made about the run of "Abie's Irish Rose" was that it would "probably run forever." I did refer to it guardedly as the "worst play of the season" (June, 1922) but also remarked, "Probably what the American public wants, God forbid," a quotation which was used by the management on the front of the theatre, with "God Forbid" omitted.

So shut up!

The New Yorker, December 23, 1939

THE MALE AND ALLIED ANIMALS

J AMES THURBER, with his unique talents and wide following, must expect, when he writes a play in the conventional idiom of the theatre, to be beset by two types of zealot: (a) those Thurber fans who don't find enough Thurber in his play and (b) those Thurber fans who detect too much. (There was one dope sitting up back at the opening of "The Male Animal" who was so anxious not to miss the Thurber Touch that he screamed at every line just to be on the safe side.)

In spite of our editorial proximity, this department is not privy to Mr. Thurber's dearest wish in connection with this play which he has written with Elliott Nugent, but I have a feeling that the idea was to write a play as amusing and successful as possible about a guy who, slightly tortured within himself for no reason, insists on torturing his wife and friends with steely-eyed, searching analyses of their perfectly innocent behavior until he has managed to raise quite a lot of hell all over the place. I may be doing Mr. Thurber and Mr. Nugent an injustice, but that's what it looks like to me, and they have done a good job of it. "The Male Animal" is certainly a highly amusing and, I am sure, successful play about just that.

I also like to think that the injection of the question of academic freedom, exemplified by the young professor's determination to read Bartolomeo Vanzetti's classic valedictory aloud to his class in the face of the trustees of the new stadium was not a mere tablespoonful of sizing to give the play a semblance of shape but a genuine belief on the part of the authors that academic freedom and Bartolomeo Vanzetti's letter are worth bringing up, even in the despised medium of comedy. I'll bet that they do more good than many a preachment on a bare stage with bad actors walking around all hunched over.

And there are certainly no bad actors in "The Male Animal." Herman Shumlin has assembled and directed a practically perfect cast. Mr. Nugent, the co-author, plays the intense young professor with a humorous tenderness which brings out all the triumphant futility of the embattled male who confuses himself with the embattled female just enough to save the day for himself. Leon Ames, as the ex-football star who comes back to college "just to see a football game" and finds himself the heavy in a domestic drama with sociological undertones, is a constant delight to everyone but himself, as is young Robert Scott, the undergraduate editor who precipitates most of the trouble and builds himself a sterling bun as a consequence. Ruth Matteson has to face what any Thurber woman would have to face in the manic-depressive gamut and does it nobly, and little Miss Gene Tierney is without doubt pretty enough to have caused her end of the mess. It is also good to see Ivan Simpson back from Hollywood in the rôle of the dean who just wants to go and lie down, and I hope that a lot of trustees see and ponder on Matt Briggs' performance.

If you, as a Thurber fan, go to see "The Male Animal" expecting to find a counterpart of the Thurber fish with hysterical ears or the gull who "cannot get his head down any further than this," you may be confused for an act or so, for those particular flights of the Thurber imagination (if it really is imagination) have been held in check to conform with the limits of Aristotle's unities and by the fact that there are some things too sacred even for the theatre. But if you have recognized the down-to-earth understanding of strictly human problems of behavior, tinctured with a scorn for those who are cocksure that they have solved them, which marks the Thurber drawings and writings, then you will warm to this delightful comedy, which, with Mr. Nugent's practical coöperation, has, I am proud to say, come out of this office.

The New Yorker, January 20, 1940

ONE THING AND ANOTHER

HAVING put the Creative Urge on ice in "Kindred," our good friends from Eire have wisely gone back to "Juno and the Paycock," from which there can be no appeal. Every time we see it, there is something fresh to thrill to. Possibly there has crept into it a slight excess of facility in the playing, a sureness of touch which borders on jauntiness, but that is certainly nothing to cavil at. With Barry Fitzgerald and Sara Allgood at the controls, sureness of touch is inescapable, and, jaunty or not, a rare treat in acting.

There is so much of everything in Sean O'Casey's play and it has become so much a part of every theatregoing gourmet's menu that all that is necessary to add at this time is that it is here done, by the Fitzgerald-Allgood combination, at its best, with possible reservations about some of the minor rôles. If you are familiar with it, you don't need to be told any more. If you are not, I envy you your first acquaintance.

Once an author has named his play "The Man Who Killed Lincoln" he has more or less tipped his mitt. He could almost call the whole thing off right there, as far as any suspense goes. The success of his venture depends entirely on how many people want to sit in a theatre and watch a man impersonating John Wilkes Booth shoot a man impersonating Lincoln, and then follow him down as far as the Garrett farm, where, unless certain rumors are to be believed, he himself is killed.

Elmer Harris and Philip Van Doren Stern (the latter the author of the book from which the play was made) might have done better if they had taken these rumors as a springboard and gone into speculation as to what might have happened to Booth if he had escaped. If memory serves me, the career of John St. Helen, whether he was Booth or not, could have been made into a fairly fascinating play. And fascinating the late opus was not, in spite of the fact that it was obviously a sincere attempt.

There can hardly be any criticism of Richard Waring's playing Booth as a ham, considering what Booth was. Although I never saw Booth plain, I should say that Mr. Waring gave a very good visual characterization and the histrionics we must put down to fidelity to history. The most believable performance, however, possibly because it expressed what everyone was aching to say, was that of Whitford Kane, who told Booth off in good Dixie Irish in the character of Samuel Cox. I am afraid that "The Man Who Killed Lincoln" was just what you would expect it to have been.

THERE are certain risks entailed in dramatic criticism that you boys and girls, sitting in your warm, comfortable drawing rooms, do not dream of. To take an instance (the only one I have at hand): I attended the opening of Uncle Sam's Music Hall some weeks ago with my family, or as much of it as we could get at one table. It so turned out that the show was not only dull but extraordinarily offensive (a feature which I understand was eliminated the following night), and on my way out, slightly before the scheduled hour, I took occasion to deliver a short lecture to the producer on the sidewalk in front of his theatre. My argument that his show was not one which a father could take his children to was slightly vitiated by the fact that the child in question was at that moment towering over me from a height of six foot two and was accompanied by his wife, but my point was technically correct and I made the most of it. In fact, I lashed out.

Last week, in Danton Walker's column in the *Daily News*, appeared the following not-so-cryptic item:

> What litterateur, occasional radio comic and whilom dramatic critic was tossed bodily from Harry Bannister's jernt (Uncle Sam's Music Hall) for being drunk and disorderly?

Both Mr. Bannister and Mr. Walker express pained surprise that anything personal should have been read into this innocent reference, and I would not bring the matter up except for that word "whilom." That's what hurts.

—ROBERT BENCHLEY

The New Yorker, January 27, 1940